W9-BAZ-950

ULYSSES S. GRANT

AND THE STRATEGY OF VICTORY

THE HISTORY OF THE CIVIL WAR

THE HISTORY OF THE CIVIL WAR

ULYSSES S. GRANT

AND THE STRATEGY OF VICTORY

by LAURA ANN RICKARBY

INTRODUCTORY ESSAY BY
HENRY STEELE COMMAGER

SILVER BURDETT PRESS

In memory of Jacob Schlesinger, with love

The author wishes to express special thanks to Professors Alden Vaughan and Eric Foner of Columbia University for their mentorship, guidance, and patience.

Series Editorial Supervisor: Richard G. Gallin
Series Editing: Agincourt Press
Series Consultant: Elizabeth Fortson
Cover and Text Design: Circa 86, New York
Series Supervision of Art and Design: Leslie Bauman
Maps: Susan Johnston Carlson

Consultants: Rudy Johnson, Social Studies Coordinator, Lansing Public Schools, Lansing, Michigan; Arnold Markoe, Professor, Brooklyn College, City University of New York.

Library of Congress Cataloging-in-Publication Data
Rickarby, Laura Ann
    Ulysses S. Grant and the strategy of victory / by Laura Ann Rickarby.
      p.   cm. — (The History of the Civil War)
    Includes bibliograpical references (p.   ).
    Summary: A biography of war hero and President Ulysses S. Grant
    1. Grant, Ulysses S. (Ulysses Simpson), 1822-1885—Juvenile literature. 2. Generals—United States—Biography—Juvenile literature. 3. United States. Army—Biography—Juvenile literature. 4. United States—History—Civil War, 1861-1865—Campaigns—Juvenile literature. 5. United States—History—War with Mexico, 1845-1848—Campaigns—Juvenile literature. 6. Presidents—United States—Biography—Juvenile literature. [1. Grant, Ulysses S. (Ulysses Simpson), 1822-1885. 2. Generals. 3. Presidents. 4. United States—History—Civil War, 1861-1865.] I. Title. II. Series.
E672.R53 1990
973.8′2′092—dc20
[B]
[92]
ISBN 0-382-09944-3 (lib. bdg.)   ISBN 0-382-24053-7 (pbk.)

90-32370
CIP
AC

TABLE OF CONTENTS

The baby born in the little village of Mount Pleasant, Ohio, in the spring of 1822 to Captain Jesse Grant and Hanna Simpson was destined to become one of the greatest warriors this nation has ever known. Though his parents were of course unaware of their son's glorious future, they did give him a name that would prove prophetic: Ulysses Simpson, which would allow him to be known as U.S. Grant. No better name than that for a young man determined to be a soldier.

At the age of 15, Ulysses applied to West Point and was duly accepted. From that time to the end of his life he was a soldier. Young Ulysses had learned to handle horse back on the family farm, a skill that stood him in good stead at West Point and throughout his long career in the military. He turned out to be a good enough student at the military academy, and a horseman without peer.

After graduating from the Point in 1843 he received a commission in the cavalry, but was soon shifted to the infantry. With the Mexican War he saw active service. He admired General Zachary Taylor, in command of the army on the Mexican border, and never forgot that General Taylor went from the saddle to the White House. In those early years, the army provided rapid promotion. Soon there was a young Captain Grant. As the best horseman in his regiment he distinguished himself both for his enterprise and his courage. Transferred to General Winfield Scott's command, he fought at Vera Cruz and then in the attack on Mexico City. The ample fighting he saw was a preparation for his future.

During the postwar years Grant saw service first in New York and then, by way of Panama, in San Francisco. Bored with service on the Pacific coast, he resigned from the army—a resignation accepted by the then secretary of war Jefferson Davis, and doubtless one he lived to regret. Once out of the army, he dabbled in real estate, engineering, the customs service, and in the leather business in Galena, Illinois, which was quite a comedown.

With the secession of the South, everything changed. The governor of Illinois appointed him a colonel of the 21st Illinois volunteers, which he whipped into shape with great efficiency. Ordered to Missouri, he was appointed a brigadier general. Within a short time Grant's command grew to 20,000. Eager for action, he moved his army south into what Confederates believed was their territory.

Nothing daunted Grant. He once again took the offensive, this time pushing deep into Confederate territory. His objective was two powerful forts, Donelson and Henry, on the Cumberland and Tennessee rivers. These strong Confederate forts closed both rivers. Grant's troops battered the Confederates, drove them out of their trenches, and confronted them with inevitable defeat. To the Confederate commander Grant gave the simplest of terms: unconditional surrender. That attitude came to be typical of Grant's entire Civil War career.

It would be impossible here to do more than sketch Grant's four years of war. He was always ready to seize the offensive. He captured Vicksburg, which was supposed to be invulnerable, and thus closed much of the trans-Mississippi West to the Confederacy. He held his own at Antietam, where Lee suffered irreparable losses, and again at Gettysburg. He took over command of the grand strategy of the war, and inflicted on the Confederates losses they simply could not stand. Victory came hard, but it came in the end in large part because Grant imposed it on the Confederates. When Lee finally surrendered the Confederate army at Appomattox, Grant made sure that all Rebel soldiers could keep their rifles, their horses, and whatever they might need for rebuilding their farms and their communities. He was, with Lee, not only a military genius, but a great and noble leader.

It was a foregone conclusion that the reunited nation would send U.S. Grant to the White House. Together he and Lincoln had won the war. Together they had reunited the Union. Together they had freed the slaves and forever ended slavery. Grant was elected to the presidency in 1968, and at 46 was one of the youngest men ever to hold that office. It was not his most distinguished achievement, however. History would always remember Grant as the determined man of the hour who pressed the Union to victory.

CIVIL WAR TIME LINE

May 22
Kansas-Nebraska Act states that in new territories the question of slavery will be decided by the citizens. Many Northerners are outraged because this act could lead to the extension of slavery.

1854   **1855**   **1856**   **1857**

May 21
Lawrence, Kansas is sacked by proslavery Missourians.
May 22
Senator Charles Sumner is caned by Preston Brooks for delivering a speech against slavery.
May 24 – 25
Pottawatomie Creek massacre committed by John Brown and four of his sons.

March 6
The Supreme Court, in the *Dred Scott* ruling, declares that blacks are not U. S. citizens, and therefore cannot bring lawsuits. The ruling divides the country on the question of the legal status of blacks.

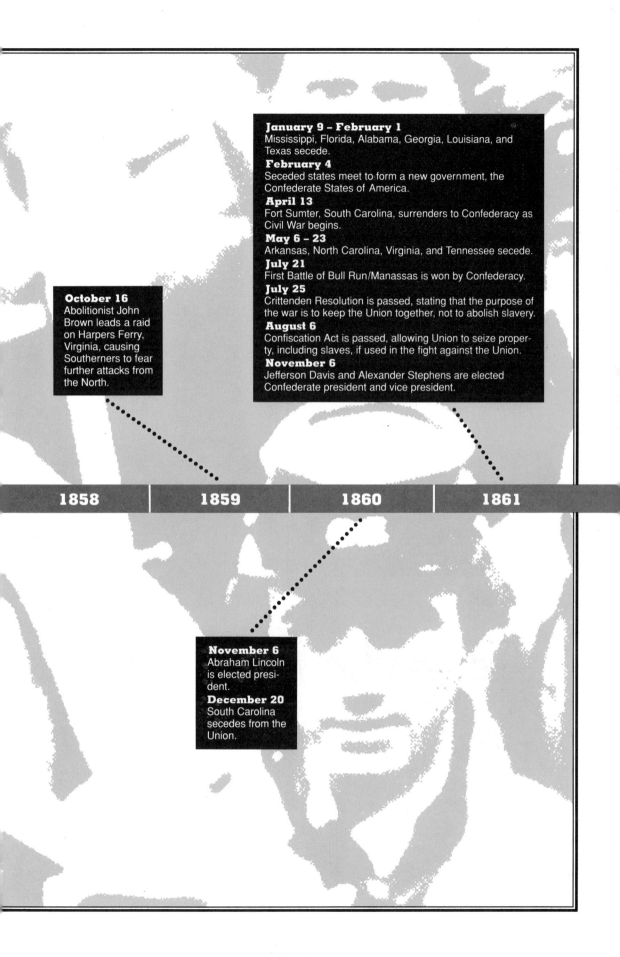

January 9 – February 1
Mississippi, Florida, Alabama, Georgia, Louisiana, and Texas secede.

February 4
Seceded states meet to form a new government, the Confederate States of America.

April 13
Fort Sumter, South Carolina, surrenders to Confederacy as Civil War begins.

May 6 – 23
Arkansas, North Carolina, Virginia, and Tennessee secede.

July 21
First Battle of Bull Run/Manassas is won by Confederacy.

July 25
Crittenden Resolution is passed, stating that the purpose of the war is to keep the Union together, not to abolish slavery.

August 6
Confiscation Act is passed, allowing Union to seize property, including slaves, if used in the fight against the Union.

November 6
Jefferson Davis and Alexander Stephens are elected Confederate president and vice president.

October 16
Abolitionist John Brown leads a raid on Harpers Ferry, Virginia, causing Southerners to fear further attacks from the North.

1858   **1859**   **1860**   **1861**

November 6
Abraham Lincoln is elected president.

December 20
South Carolina secedes from the Union.

February 6
Fort Henry, Tennessee, is captured.

February 16
Fort Donelson, Tennessee, is captured by Union.

March 9
Monitor and *Merrimack* battle near Hampton Roads, Virginia.

March 23
Shenandoah Valley Campaign opens with Union victory over Maj. Gen. Thomas J. "Stonewall" Jackson.

April 7
Gen. Ulysses S. Grant wins Battle of Shiloh, Tennessee, splitting rebel forces on the Mississippi River.

April 25
New Orleans is captured by Union naval forces led by flag officer David Farragut.

June 19
Slavery is abolished in U. S. territories.

June 25
Gen. Robert E. Lee leads rout of Gen. George McClellan's army in the Seven Days Battles.

July 17
The United States Congress authorizes formation of the first black regiments.

August 29 – 30
Second Battle of Bull Run/Manassas is won by Confederacy.

September 5
Lee leads first Confederate invasion of the North into Maryland.

September 17
Battle of Antietam/Sharpsburg, bloodiest of the war, ends in a stalemate between Lee and McClellan.

| 1862 | 1863 | 1864 | 1865 |

January 1
Lincoln issues Emancipation Proclamation, freeing slaves in Confederate states.

March 3
U.S. Congress passes its first military draft.

April 2
Bread riots occur in Richmond, Virginia.

May 1 – 4
Battle of Chancellorsville is won by Confederacy; Stonewall Jackson is accidentally shot by his own troops.

May 22 – July 4
Union wins siege of Vicksburg in Mississippi.

June 3
Lee invades the North from Fredericksburg, Virginia.

July 3
Battle of Gettysburg is won in Pennsylvania by Union.

July 13 – 17
Riots occur in New York City over the draft.

November 19
Lincoln delivers the Gettysburg Address.

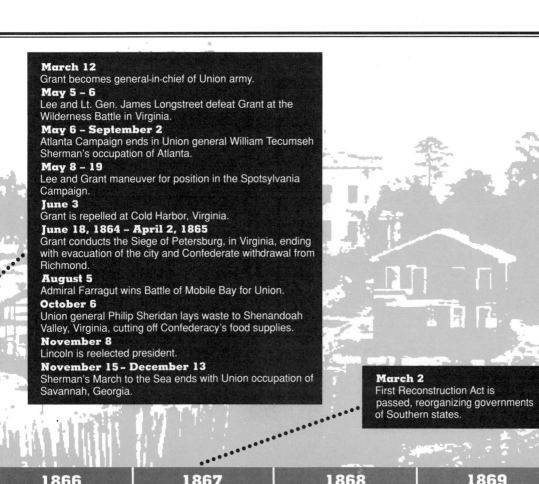

March 12
Grant becomes general-in-chief of Union army.
May 5 – 6
Lee and Lt. Gen. James Longstreet defeat Grant at the Wilderness Battle in Virginia.
May 6 – September 2
Atlanta Campaign ends in Union general William Tecumseh Sherman's occupation of Atlanta.
May 8 – 19
Lee and Grant maneuver for position in the Spotsylvania Campaign.
June 3
Grant is repelled at Cold Harbor, Virginia.
June 18, 1864 – April 2, 1865
Grant conducts the Siege of Petersburg, in Virginia, ending with evacuation of the city and Confederate withdrawal from Richmond.
August 5
Admiral Farragut wins Battle of Mobile Bay for Union.
October 6
Union general Philip Sheridan lays waste to Shenandoah Valley, Virginia, cutting off Confederacy's food supplies.
November 8
Lincoln is reelected president.
November 15 – December 13
Sherman's March to the Sea ends with Union occupation of Savannah, Georgia.

March 2
First Reconstruction Act is passed, reorganizing governments of Southern states.

1866	1867	1868	1869

April 9
Civil Rights Act of 1866 is passed. Among other things, it removes states' power to keep former slaves from testifying in court or owning property.

November 3
Ulysses S. Grant is elected president.

January 31
Thirteenth Amendment, freeing slaves, is passed by Congress and sent to states for ratification.
February 1 – April 26
Sherman invades the Carolinas.
February 6
Lee is appointed general-in-chief of Confederate armies.
March 3
Freedman's Bureau is established to assist former slaves.
April 9
Lee surrenders to Grant at Appomattox Courthouse, Virginia.
April 15
Lincoln dies from assassin's bullet; Andrew Johnson becomes president.
May 26
Remaining Confederate troops surrender.

UNCONDITIONAL SURRENDER

"The one who attacks first now will be
victorious...."

GRANT AT FORT DONELSON

ashington, D.C., January 1862—The Civil War is 10 months old, and President Abraham Lincoln is growing frustrated with his generals. He had hoped to crush the Southern rebellion quickly. Instead, the Union armies have suffered a humiliating defeat in the Battle of Bull Run. General George McClellan, whom Lincoln made commander, is proving to be a slow, careful leader. McClellan seems to spend all his time planning battles rather than fighting them. Finally Lincoln sends him a humorous but edgy note: If General McClellan is not using his army, the president would like to borrow it for a while.

McClellan promises to act soon. In 10 days, he declares, his Army of the Potomac will invade the Confederate capital of Richmond. But 10 days pass, and the army is still camped in Washington. Lincoln considers removing McClellan from command. But where can he find a general who will fight?

Deafening blasts sounded as the first shells pounded into the walls of Fort Donelson. The men on the Union ships cheered the hits. Flag officer Andrew Foote, commanding the naval attack on the Tennessee fort, then ordered his ships in closer. He wanted to fire from point-blank range.

No sooner did the ships move in than the guns from the fort opened fire. Shells ripped through the Union squadron, damaging two ships and killing dozens of men. Foote himself was badly injured. He called off the attack and sent word to the army commander on shore that it had failed.

The commander did not have to be told. He had watched the whole thing from the banks of the Cumberland River. He was a short, scruffy man, who usually plodded up and down the ragged lines of his troops with the stump of a cigar in his mouth. He was not a well-known general like McClellan, who was renowned for his strategy, but he knew what had to be done. The navy had failed. The army would have to take the fort on its own.

There was no other option for a man like Ulysses S. Grant. He did not believe in delay. If the Union troops could take Fort Donelson, the Confederate forces would be driven out of Tennessee and the whole West would be opened up. It would be a crippling blow to the South. Therefore it must be done, no matter how.

Most generals of the time followed their hero, the French conqueror Napoleon, in strategy. They planned every detail of a battle carefully, trying to guess each step the enemy would take. Then they carried out their plans to the letter. But Grant believed in seizing the moment. If new circumstances arose, he would change his plans to take advantage of them.

Grant's army was positioned in a semicircle on one side of the fort. The river was on the other side. The Rebels were not going anywhere. Grant figured he had some time to think about a plan of attack.

But the 17,000 Confederate troops inside had other ideas. Their commanders decided to make a break for it. On the icy cold morning of February 15, a cry went up from the right flank of the Union forces. The crackle of musket fire sounded through the thicket of trees that hugged the riverbank. The Rebels were attacking!

The Union troops dropped their breakfast plates and picked up their guns. They ran for cover and returned the fire. A frantic note was sent off to the farmhouse where General Grant had set up his headquarters, telling him that the Rebels were making a break for it. But the messenger came back with shocking news: The general was not there.

In fact, Grant, not suspecting an attack, had gone aboard Foote's ship to check the damage to the squadron. Now the entire right side of the Union army was being driven toward the center. The Rebels were breaking a hole in the ranks. Nearly 1,500 men had been killed already, and the inexperienced Union troops were fleeing in panic. Soon all the Confederate troops would be able to escape from the fort.

General John McClernand, whose troops had been wiped out, held a frantic meeting with several other officers to decide what should be done. Just than a horse came charging into their midst, and a man dismounted. He had a wide face half-covered by a dirty red beard. It was General Grant, and he looked angry.

"The army wants a head," McClernand said nervously. McClernand had little experience of war. He had been an Illinois congressman before Lincoln made him a general.

"It seems so," Grant growled. He was upset with himself for planning his next move and not expecting this attack. If he did not act soon, his army would be driven away and the Confederates would escape. That would be the end of the military career of Ulysses S. Grant.

It was time for some quick thinking. Grant had seen that the attacking Confederates had full sacks on their backs. This meant that they did not intend to go back to the fort. Just now the battlefield had grown quiet. The guns of the attackers fell silent as they regrouped. Grant turned to his officers and said, "Some of our men are pretty badly demoralized, but the enemy must be more so, for he has attempted to force his way out but has fallen back; the one who attacks first now will be victorious."

Grant barked out a series of orders. The left side of the line would mount an all-out attack on the weakest part of the

Confederate forces. Messengers ran off in all directions. The officers sped to their commands. General Charles F. Smith, a tough old soldier who had once been Grant's commander at West Point Military Acadamy, led the counterattack.

Just as Grant had thought, the Rebel troops were exhausted and discouraged after their attack. They retreated into the fort in the face of the strong counterattack. Dozens were killed. As night came on, the Union forces held the field once again. Now, thought Grant, it was only a matter of time before those inside surrendered.

That night the temperature dropped. Men huddled in the open fields or trotted in circles to keep warm. Grant had forbidden them to light campfires, which would make the enemy aware of their positions. He was not taking more chances. The soldiers ate a crude dinner and talked hopefully about the battle being over soon. The wounded lay in abandoned barns, moaning in the cold air as they were tended by doctors.

In his headquarters, Grant received a visitor. General Smith entered the room, kicking ice from his boots. The old warrior held out a letter. Grant read it.

The commander of the Confederate fort was Brigadier General Gideon Pillow. Pillow had determined that the Union troops had won the battle, but he himself feared capture. Therefore, he and his second in command had secretly escaped. The next man in command was Brigadier General Simon Buckner. It was Buckner who now sent a note to Grant asking for terms of surrender.

Grant knew Buckner. Buckner had once lent Grant money when Grant was down on his luck. But that was a long time ago, and this was war. Grant snapped a reply: "No terms except unconditional and immediate surrender can be accepted. I propose to move immediately upon your works."

The next morning, more than 15,000 Confederate troops laid down their arms and surrendered. When Grant met Buckner, he told him that he would lend his new prisoner as much money as he had, should he need it. The battle was over. They were done fighting and Grant could afford to be kind.

The taking of Fort Donelson was a smashing victory. The news spread fast. Throughout the North, newspapers carried the story of the first big victory of the war. Grant's gruff note to Buckner became famous. People joked that Grant's initials, "U. S." stood for "unconditional surrender."

President Lincoln got a full report on the hardheaded tactics of Grant. He was not yet ready to give up on McClellan, but he would keep in mind this fighting general from Ohio, U. S. Grant.

THE BOY FROM OHIO

"My family is American and has been for generations...."

ULYSSES S. GRANT

lysses was the name of a famous hero of Greek mythology. Ulysses fought bravely in the Trojan War, helping to bring the Greeks to victory. He was the craftiest of all the Greek warriors. Perhaps that was why Hannah Grant and her stepmother wanted to give the name Ulysses to Hannah's newborn son.

The baby was born on April 27, 1822, in a small house on the river in Point Pleasant, Ohio. Hannah was a reserved woman from a western family, the Simpsons, who owned 600 acres of land. Jesse Grant, the boy's father, was a tanner, who turned animal hides into leather.

When the Grants' first child was born, he had no name for six weeks because his parents could not decide on one. Legend has it that the Grant and Simpson families finally decided the matter by putting their choices for the baby's name on slips of paper. One piece of paper would be pulled out of a hat. The name Ulysses, suggested by Hannah's stepmother, was pulled out.

Grandfather Simpson became upset that his choice, Hiram, had not been picked. The family decided to make him happy by calling the baby Hiram Ulysses Grant. But Hannah was not happy with

the name, and so she called her child Ulysses. Years later, when the boy entered military school, his name would be changed again.

A year after Ulysses' birth, the Grants moved to Georgetown, Ohio. Ulysses spent the next 16 years of his life there. His five brothers and sisters were born there: Samuel Simpson, Clara Rachel, Virginia Pane, Orvil Lynch, and Mary Frances.

Ulysses was an ordinary boy who liked games and worked hard. "Everyone in Georgetown, Ohio worked," he said later. At about 11 years of age, Ulysses learned to work a plow. For the next several years he learned the skills of the farm. He plowed the fields, planted corn and potatoes, and used horses to haul wood. He especially liked to work with horses, and he dreamed of owning someday.

One day Ulysses heard that a neighbor named Mr. Ralston had a colt that he would be willing to sell. Ulysses begged his father to buy it for him. Mr. Ralston wanted $25 for the colt, but Mr. Grant though it was worth only $20. He finally agreed to let Ulysses bargain for the horse. Jesse Grant told his son to go to Mr. Ralston and offer $20. If Mr. Ralston would not accept that amount, Ulysses was told to offer him $22.50. If Mr. Ralston still would not budge, then the boy was to agree to pay $25.

But Ulysses did not understand the point of bargaining. He went to Mr. Ralston's house and told the man, "Papa says I may offer you twenty dollars for the colt, but if you won't take that, I am to offer twenty-two and a half, and if you won't take that, to give you twenty-five."

When the neighborhood boys heard about Ulysses's "bargaining," they laughed and called him a fool. Ulysses was shy and often felt uncomfortable when he was the center of attention. The teasing only made matters worse.

Highlights in the Life of Ulysses S. Grant

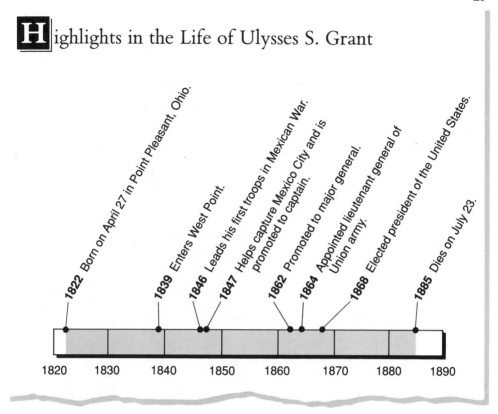

However, Ulysses did fairly well in school and was especially good at math. His only complaint was that the math he was taught was very limited. He quickly mastered it and hungered for more.

After school Ulysses was supposed to work for his father in the tannery, but he hated the place. The tanning process made the place smell awful, and Ulysses would do anything to get out of it. He was happy to chop wood, repair fences, and help around the house. Whenever he could, he rode his colt. He had a natural aptitude for horseback riding and soon became quite expert at it.

Jesse Grant knew his son had no wish to be a tanner. He decided it would be best for the boy to get a good education. He wanted a secure career for his son. He thought Ulysses might make a good engineer. This was the 1830s, and roads, bridges, and buildings were being constructed at a feverish pace as the United States expanded. There was a great demand for engineers to design and oversee such projects.

When Ulysses was 17 years old, Jesse Grant wrote to his congressman, Thomas Hamer, asking him to recommend Ulysses for a place at the United States Military Academy at West Point. There, the boy would get a first-rate education. Jesse probably also had an idea that Ulysses might become a soldier. Jesse's father, Noah Grant, had joined the Continental Army at the outbreak of the American Revolution. And Jesse's grandfather had fought in the Seven Years War that had begun in 1756. So a long military tradition existed in the Grant family. Perhaps the boy would follow it.

As it turned out, four boys from Grant's hometown of Georgetown, Ohio, had entered West Point in 1837. One of those boys dropped out in January 1838, so there was an opening. In the winter of 1838–39, Ulysses Grant was accepted. But when the boy heard the news, he was not especially pleased. He did not care for the idea of military training. He told his father he thought he would not go.

Jesse Grant became stern and said he thought Ulysses would go. The father's word was final. In the spring of 1839, Ulysses Grant prepared for the trip to New York. Like it or not, he was entering West Point.

MILITARY APPRENTICE

"Soldier! Will you work?"
AN OHIO BOY, TO ULYSSES GRANT

Ulysses reported to West Point on May 29, 1839. There he found that his name had been changed in the school's records. The papers at the academy listed him as Ulysses S. Grant. When the congressman filed his application, he had assumed that "Ulysses" was the boy's first name and that his mother's maiden name, Simpson was his middle name. Ulysses tried for a while to have the records changed, but he finally decided that he liked the new name. So Hiram Ulysses Grant became Ulysses S. Grant. In later life, he would claim that the "S" did not stand for anything.

Within two weeks, he had passed his entrance examinations, which included such subjects as math, geography, and French. Then the real work began. Grant's day as a new cadet began at 5:00 A.M. and lasted up to 12 hours. In the wintertime, the boys were allowed to sleep until 6:00 A.M.

West Point was the most famous military school in the nation. Cadets had trained there on the banks of the Hudson River in New York State since 1778, when the American Revolution was being fought. It was formally founded by Congress in 1802.

By the time Ulysses Grant entered, West Point was considered the army's officer training ground. Others who attended West Point at about the same time as Grant included Robert E. Lee, Thomas J. "Stonewall" Jackson, William Tecumseh Sherman, and George McClellan. All of these men would become famous generals in the Civil War. At West Point they were classmates, but in the war they would pit their wits against one another. Over half the West Point graduates would join the Confederate Army.

At first Ulysses hated West Point. The training was hard, the day was long, and the other boys were unfriendly. It was a tradition for upperclassmen to tease and harass the new students so as to toughen them. The shy boy from Ohio did not take well to the treatment. He became even more quiet and dreamed of leaving the academy.

Also, Ulysses was sharply aware of differences in social standing. He was a simple farm boy from Ohio. Many of his classmates were from wealthy families in New England and Virginia, where good breeding was considered essential. The parents of these young men believed that a military career was a noble one. The boys came to West Point with expensive clothes, servants, large allowances, and an attitude of born superiority. The shy tanner's son from Ohio tried his best to stay in the shadows.

Ulysses showed his unhappiness by refusing to follow the academy's many rules. Any cadet who broke the strict code of behavior or who was sloppy or late for class received marks against him, called demerits. Grant received so many demerits during his career at West Point that at one point his rank was lowered from sergeant to private.

It was important for young military apprentices to get to know useful people who could help them in their careers. Grant, however, had no natural instinct for making such contacts. He had few friends at school.

The hardest part of the day for the boy was training drill. He especially hated marching drills. He did not have natural rhythm, and he constantly marched out of step. According to legend, his superiors originally promoted him to cadet sergeant so that he

would be at the head of the column and they would not have to look at the awful way he marched beside the other men.

Life was hard and unpleasant for Ulysses at West Point, but slowly he began to adapt to it. After his first year, he made some friends. He lived and worked hard with these other boys, and they became very close. This was just the sort of experience a cadet was supposed to get from West Point. It was essential for a cadet to build ties with his classmates. Later in life, they would serve together in the military and perhaps risk their lives for one another.

As Ulysses took to the cadet's life, he came to enjoy some of his training and studies. He learned how to read maps, how to fight using musket and bayonet, how to ride horseback during a battle, how to march, and how to wear a uniform properly. He quickly shone as an expert horseman.

In school, he found few subjects to his liking. Art lessons helped improve his ability to draw battle plans. He did very well in math, and his lessons helped him to calculate such things as the amount of supplies an army in the field needed. He also studied French. It was considered necessary for the boys to learn French so that they could translate the military plans of the great French general Napoleon. Napoleon had conquered Europe 30 years before, using a combination of skill and daring. He was the most respected military leader of the age.

A cadet's career at West Point lasted for four years. Ulysses Grant finished his term ranked 21st in his class of 39. It was not a very distinguished record, but at least he had graduated and was now eligible to enter the army as an officer.

Upon graduation, each cadet was asked to choose the military unit he wanted to serve in. Grant loved horses, so he was eager to join the cavalry. However, at the time he graduated there was only one cavalry unit in the army. There was keen competition for the few openings, and since Grant had not done well in his studies, he was not considered. He would have to join the infantry, which was composed of soldiers who fought on foot.

Still, he had at least graduated, and was now a brevet second lieutenant—that is, he was given the title of second lieutenant, although he was still paid as if his rank were lower. He was proud to be a military man. He had decided that the army would be his profession. He wore the uniform proudly when he went back to his hometown. He hoped to impress his old schoolmates and, he later said, "especially the girls."

One day shortly after graduation, Grant happened to be riding through the streets of Cincinnati, Ohio. He thought he looked quite grand sitting tall on his horse in his dignified uniform. Suddenly a poor, scruffy-looking boy appeared on the street and yelled at him as he rode past, "Soldier! Will you work? No, siree; I'll sell my shirt first!"

This insulting remark struck the proud young officer. He suddenly felt ridiculous parading through the streets in his fancy uniform past poor children wearing only rags. Grant later said that this single event gave him a dislike for military finery that would always remain with him. Years later as a Civil War general, he would often appear on the battlefield wearing a tattered private's uniform.

Grant was now assigned to Jefferson Barracks outside St. Louis, Missouri. One of Grant's best friends at West Point had been Frederick Dent, whose family owned a farm called White Haven near St. Louis. Grant visited his friend's family often after graduation and soon fell in love with Dent's 18-year-old sister, Julia. Whereas Ulysses Grant was shy, Julia was lively and outgoing. The two went horseback riding together and went on long walks in the woods. Grant felt great love for the girl, but he was too shy to ask if she felt the same.

Then a change came. The year was 1844. Rumors of war were in the air. Newspapers said it was only a matter of time before the United States declared war on Mexico. The two nations had been exchanging heated words over the question of Texas. The United States wanted to admit Texas as a new state. Mexico considered it part of its territory. President John Tyler issued a call for troops at the Texas border. The Fourth Infantry Regiment, Grant's regiment, received orders to move.

The idea of separation moved Grant to act. He dashed out of White Haven just before his regiment was due to leave, told Julia he loved her, and asked if she would marry him. She accepted. They became engaged and promised to marry when Ulysses returned.

WAR WITH MEXICO

"There is no great sport in having bullets fly
about one in every direction..."

ULYSSES S. GRANT TO HIS WIFE, JULIA

The United States in the 1840s was swept by a fever called Manifest Destiny. The Revolutionary period was long over, and the brash young country was exercising its muscle. Settlers were spreading farther and farther west, staking claims on land that had once belonged to American Indians. The feeling was that the "empire of freedom" (the United States of America) needed to expand its boundaries. The nation's western boundaries extended only about halfway across the continent. That was not good enough.

In 1845, the newspaper editor John Louis O'Sullivan summed up the popular feeling. "Our manifest destiny," he wrote, "is to overspread the continent allotted by Providence for the free development of our yearly multiplying millions." Americans considered it their God-given right to take over the continent, no matter what stood in the way.

The native Americans stood in the way, but the tribes were scattered and fairly easy to conquer. A bigger problem was that much of the western land that American settlers were pouring into was owned by Mexico.

The first big argument arose over Texas. Texas had been a part of Mexico when Mexico won its independence from Spain in 1821. But the area had few people living in it, so in 1824 the Mexican government gave permission for some Americans to settle there. The Mexican government insisted that the settlers become Roman Catholics. Within a few years, however, the American settlers of Texas began to act as though the Mexican government did not exist. They tried to set up their own government in Texas and ignored the laws of Mexico. In addition, by 1830, the Mexican government was alarmed by the fact that 20,000 American settlers had brought more than 1,000 slaves into Texas. Mexico had outlawed slavery. For these reasons, the Mexican government demanded a stop to all American immigration into Texas.

In 1834, General Antonio Lopez de Santa Anna seized power in Mexico. He dissolved the National Congress, abolished the federal system, and set himself up as dictator. Two years later, the Texans set up their own government. Santa Anna stormed into Texas with an army of several thousand men and attacked the fortified mission in San Antonio called the Alamo, killing all of its 187 defenders. The legendary frontiersmen Jim Bowie and Davy Crockett died defending the fort.

Forty days later, the Texas patriot Sam Houston led an army of more than 700 men against Santa Anna at the San Jacinto River. In a battle that lasted only 18 minutes, Houston and his men killed more than 600 Mexican soldiers and took an equal number prisoner, including General Santa Anna. In exchange for his freedom, Santa Anna agreed to sign a treaty recognizing Texas as an independent republic.

Texas continued as an independent republic for the next nine years, but then asked to be admitted to the United States. Many Americans did not want the United States to annex Texas. Some feared that such an action would lead to war with Mexico. Others thought that admitting Texas to the United States would strengthen slavery. Opposition was especially strong in the Northeast. Many there feared that Texas would be carved up into four or five slave states. Finally, however, the U.S. Congress approved the annexation. On December 29, 1845, Texas became the 28th state.

This action angered the Mexican government. Many officials in Mexico City never considered Santa Anna's forced treaty legal. They considered Texas still a part of Mexico. Representatives of the Mexican government complained to President James K. Polk. But Polk was committed to U.S. expansion. He responded to the crisis by ordering troops to the border. Ulysses Grant was among these troops.

Another argument concerned the exact boundary between Mexico and the United States. The Mexicans said that it was the Nueces River, while the Americans said it was the Rio Grande, 100 miles farther west. For this reason, President Polk ordered American troops to take up positions along the Rio Grande. General Zachary Taylor led 3,500 soldiers, half of the standing United States Army, to the river. The Mexican government sent troops to the river as well. There was a showdown. The Mexicans told General Taylor to pull his men back to the Nueces River. But General Taylor stood his ground.

In fact, President Polk had told the general to remain at the Rio Grande. He was hoping to force the Mexicans to begin fighting. Then he would have an excuse to declare war.

In April 1846, an American patrol clashed with a small number of Mexican troops. Shots were fired. It was a small encounter, but President Polk declared that American soldiers had been killed on American soil. He asked Congress to declare war.

Most members of Congress who belonged to Polk's party, the Democratic Party, supported Polk and the war, and war was declared. However, many Americans felt the war was unjust and immoral. Abraham Lincoln, who entered Congress in 1847, spoke out strongly against the war. Although Grant, as a soldier, fought in the war, he was privately against it. He and others saw the war as a way for the United States to get more land where slavery could spread.

The first real battle of the war took place on May 8, 1846, almost a week before war was officially declared. General Tyler's troops encountered the Mexican army at a place called Palo Alto. The battle lasted six hours. Grant, who was at Palo Alto that day, got his first taste of combat.

Afterward, he wrote home to Julia, "Although the balls were whizing [sic] thick and fast about me I did not feel a sensation of fear until...a ball struck close by me killing one man instantly... There is no great sport in having bullets flying about one in every direction...."

So at first the young officer experienced a natural fear in battle. Later, he discovered that once the fighting started he became calm. He found that he was a natural soldier.

Grant had a great respect for his commander, General Zachary Taylor. "A more efficient army for its number and armament I do not believe ever fought a battle than the one commanded by General Taylor in his first two engagements on Mexican-Texas soil," Grant said. On the other hand, Grant was an inexperienced lieutenant at the time, so he may not have been a great judge of military ability. But he admired the informal dress and manner of "Old Rough and Ready," as Taylor was called, and would copy them later in life.

Despite the respect Zachary Taylor had won from Grant, he did occasionally have trouble handling troops. In 1846, Taylor encamped his men just outside Matamoros. The troops plundered and committed horrible crimes. They drank in the streets of the city and shot innocent people for amusement. A regular officer wrote in his diary that "in broad light of day, not less than one hundred Mexicans were slain in cold blood, and out of about 7,000 still in town, 5,000 more or less fled." In the beginning of all this trouble, Taylor did not punish any of the soldiers who committed these crimes. Even when the situation became extremely bad, Taylor did not send the soldiers to jail. Instead, he declared it illegal to sell alcohol to American troops.

Grant's first job during the Mexican War was that of quartermaster, responsible for organizing sleeping space for the troops. He was also in charge of supplies—food, clothing, and weapons. This job kept him off the battlefield and away from the fighting. But he could not stay away.

At the Battle of Monterrey, the American troops prepared to attack the Mexican city. Grant's curiosity got the best of him. He mounted a horse and rode to the front line to see what was going on. He was there only a short time when orders were given to charge the enemy. Grant did not want to ride back to camp, so he charged along with the rest of the army.

The enemy opened fire, and one-third of the Americans were killed within minutes. Those who were not hurt quickly retreated. After the retreat, Lieutenant Charles Hoskins asked Grant if he could borrow Grant's horse. He would be better able to command the men from horseback. Lieutenant Hoskins was on the horse for only a short time before he was mowed down by enemy gunfire. Grant was ordered to take Hoskins' place and act as leader for the remaining men. This was his first time leading other men, and the chance came by pure luck.

Like Grant, Robert E. Lee distinguished himself in the Mexican War.

Grant also met up with Robert E. Lee in the Mexican War, in April 1847 at the Battle of Cerro Gordo. Lee would later become the general commander of the Confederate forces in the Civil War. The two men were part of the unit involved in the battle. Men were sent to scout out, or to make, a road for a surprise rear attack on the enemy. These scouts were led by Captain Robert E. Lee. Grant remembered Lee years later because of the efficient job Lee did as the scout commander. Lee was able to build a road without being noticed by Santa Anna or his troops. The Battle of Cerro Gordo was a swift victory for the Americans, thanks to Lee's skill and efficiency in building that road.

Another famous man whom Grant served with in Mexico was Winfield Scott. Scott would become the commander of Union forces in the early days of the Civil War. Grant looked up to Scott as an extraordinary and highly skilled leader. "General Scott's successes are an answer to all criticism," Grant wrote. "He invaded a populous country, penetrating 260 miles into the interior, with a force at no time equal to one half of that opposed to him; he was without a base; the enemy was always entrenched, always on the defensive; yet, he won every battle, he captured the capital, and conquered the government."

Grant was with General Scott in the final battle of the war, in which Scott captured the capital, Mexico City. Grant commanded a small group of soldiers in the march on the city. As they neared the city, the fighting grew fierce. Before they reached the center of the battle, Grant spotted a church on a hill. He decided that this would be a good place from which to fire guns down on the city. Grant led a few of his men in a dash for the church. Grant knocked on the door. A priest answered but would not let Grant in.

Grant spoke to the priest in Spanish. He told the priest to save the church and himself by letting the Americans in. The priest refused. Grant said that his soldiers would force their way in and probably cause destruction. Finally the priest opened the door.

The soldiers set up their guns in the lower part of the church. The shells they fired "dropped in upon the enemy and created great confusion," Grant later said. General Scott's men advanced steadily, aided by the diversion Grant had caused. Grant was later promoted to captain for the bravery he had shown in helping to capture the city.

In order to attack Mexico City, General Scott had to seize Chapultepec Hill. It was not an ordinary hill. Two hundred feet high, Chapultepec Hill was crowned by the Mexican Military College. Scott sent captains Lee and Pillow, along with lieutenants Joseph E. Johnston, Thomas Jackson (the future "Stonewall" Jackson of the Civil War), and James Longstreet, to capture the hill.

The attack on the hill was a daylong bombardment. For 14 straight hours the Americans laid shellfire upon the Military College. Finally the walls of the school began to fall down. The American soldiers then stormed the hill by using ropes to scale the school's walls. Once inside, they fought hand to hand with the young Mexican cadets—called "los Niños"—who assisted in Chapultepec's defense. These young men suffered terrible losses. The battle had been long, but successful.

After fierce fighting, the American army forced its way into the center of the city. They had taken the town. Soldiers headed for the Halls of Montezuma, the government offices. Inside, the American troops removed the Mexican officials and set up quarters.

With the taking of the capital, the Mexican War ended. President Polk sent a peace representative to discuss terms. But the Mexican government was slow to discuss a peace treaty. Mexico's leaders were still angry about the loss of the Texas territory and about President Polk's abuse of power in starting the war. Since the Mexicans refused to enter discussions, Polk called the representative back. This action caused the Mexicans to change their minds. They feared that if the representative returned to the United States, the war might start again.

The talks began on January 2, 1848. They took place in the Mexican village of Guadalupe Hidalgo, and so the treaty that was eventually worked out became known as the Treaty of Guadalupe Hidalgo. It was signed on February 2, 1848.

The conditions agreed to were as follows: Mexico was to give up all claims to Texas. Mexico also was to give the United States a huge area of land called the Mexican Cession. This included all of what would later become the states of California, Nevada, and Utah, as well as parts of Arizona, New Mexico, Wyoming, and Colorado. In exchange, the United States was to pay $15 million to Mexico. The U.S. government would also pay for any claims made by American citizens against the Mexican government for damages suffered during the war.

The part of the treaty by which the huge land area was gained was precisely what President Polk and other Manifest Destiny leaders in Washington had hoped to achieve when they started the Mexican War. The United States promised to respect the religious, political, and property rights of Mexicans living in the new lands gained in the Southwest. The U.S. boundaries now extended across the continent from the Atlantic to the Pacific Ocean.

The country paid a price for this enormous growth. Out of 78,718 Americans who served in the Mexican War, 1,733 soldiers died in battle, 4,152 were wounded, and 11,550 died of disease. The American government spent $97.7 million in the war.

But these losses were accepted. The United States was on the move.

5

ATTITUDES NORTH AND SOUTH

"We have got to deal with this slavery question, and got to give it much more attention hereafter."

ABRAHAM LINCOLN, 1848

The night of October 2, 1854, was cool and crisp in Springfield, Illinois. A great crowd had gathered around the porch of an old house to hear one of the outstanding speakers of the day. A short man with a large head, long black hair, and flashing eyes, he stood on the porch and told the people that a new day was dawning in America. Some in the crowd cheered the man; others booed. Everybody had an opinion.

The speaker was Senator Stephen Douglas, one of the cleverest and most tireless statesman of the day. He had recently gotten Congress to pass a bill concerning the new territories of the West. The moment the bill passed, it set off a storm across the nation.

The subject of the bill was slavery. Now that so much new territory had been made part of the United States, the question that concerned Americans was whether slavery should be legal in these new lands once they became states.

Generally speaking, Americans were split geographically on the slavery issue. As far back as 1819, Northerners and Southerners disagreed on the matter. Northern congressmen tended to be against the spread of slavery, and Southern congressmen tended to be in favor of it.

One way to understand why the two sides disagreed is to look at how the men and women of that day lived. Although it did have large cities, the South was basically a rural society. Landowning and farming were the major ways to make a living. At a very young age, most Southern boys learned how to ride horseback, plant crops, and hunt. In the South, the best education was one that prepared a boy to become a good farmer.

Some men in Southern society grew up in rich families. These "Southern gentlemen" inherited much wealth and went to the best

In Madison Co. Court!
LARGE SALE OF
LAND AND NEGROES

Petition for Sale of Land and Slaves.

Albert G. McClellan and others

vs.

Mary Vaden and husband, G. W. Vaden and others, distributees of Isabella McClellan, dec'd.

In the above cause, the undersigned, Clerk of the County Court of Madison county, Tenn., as commissioner, will expose to public sale on Saturday, 24th of March next, at the Court house, in the town of Jackson, that most desirable and conveniently situated Tract of Land, known as the McClellan farm, containing

1000 ACRES.

in one body, and lying within a mile and a half of the town of Jackson. Also, at the same time and place,

18 Or 20 NEGROES,

consisting of men, women and children. The land will be divided into tracts previous to the day of sale, and each division will be sold seperately.

Terms of sale.—Land on a credit of one and two years, and the negroes upon a credit of 12 months from the day of sale. Notes, with good security, will be required of purchasers, and lien retained on both land and negroes for the purchase money. Title t the land and negroes indisputable.

P. C. McCOWAT,

C. & M. Commissioner

Feb. 24, 1860.

This notice advertised a sale in Tennessee that featured "land and Negroes."

colleges. They could afford many luxuries and owned plantations. Plantations were large areas of land on which crops such as cotton were grown. Because plantations were so large, a good deal of help was needed to work the land. Southern plantation owners turned to the use of slaves for labor. Using slaves, plantation owners could produce their crops and make a profit. The operation of plantations largely came to an end after the end of slavery. It was replaced by a system that divided the land into smaller, more manageable units. These smaller areas eventually were worked by tenant farmers, who rented the land from its owners.

Whether or not Southerners had wealth, they still lived a rural life. The majority of Southerners were farmers who lived off the land. They preferred living in the country to living in the city and resisted any change in their way of life.

Northern society was a bit different. Most people in the North were also farmers, but the farms were smaller than in the South. Also, the way of life was changing faster in the North. From the 1830s on, there was a change in Northern society toward manufacturing and crafts production. Factories sprang up in Northern towns. City living was considered fast-paced, with constant change and diversity.

A labor force working outside the home for pay began to develop. Northerners increasingly found work in factories. Immigrants were arriving from Ireland, Russia, France, Sweden, and other countries. Industries such as steel provided new jobs for these new Americans. However, working conditions were often very poor. Laborers worked 12 to 16 hours a day, six days a week.

Northerners, with their changing life-style, tended to think of the South as backward. They could not understand why Southerners refused to change to keep up with the times.

Southerners had their own ideas. To them, Northerners had no respect for tradition. Southerners were happy to leave things as they were. They believed that Northern talk of change would ruin society.

The change Southern leaders feared most was the abolition of slavery. For almost as long as the South had existed, slavery had been an important part of its society. Without slave labor, plantation owners believed, they could not make a profit. However, some experts today think the plantations could have been profitable without slavery. Had the South invested in improved farm equipment and hired regular laborers, plantations could have made money without using slaves. But the big Southern farmers had gotten used to their way of life.

By the 1830s, the abolitionist movement appeared, mostly in the North. To abolish means to destroy, and abolitionists wanted to destroy the institution of slavery. They believed it was morally wrong for one human being to own another.

This kind of thinking infuriated many old-fashioned types, such as John C. Calhoun, the longtime senator from South Carolina.

John C. Calhoun remained a fiery spokesman for slaveowners' rights throughout his lifetime.

Calhoun was a frequent spokesman for the South on many matters, including the slavery issue. Northern industries, he said, had a large supply of workers and did not have to depend on slavery. Also, the North had smaller farms and a shorter growing season than the South. Slavery was not profitable in the North, so it was easy for these Northern abolitionists to demand an end to slavery.

The differences between the North and South had already become a part of the way the government worked. Slave states usually banded together in voting on major questions, just as free states did. In 1820, the Missouri territory desired to enter the United States as a new state. At the time, the number of states that allowed slavery and the number of states that did not were equal. There were two senators from each state, so a "balance of power" existed. This balance was important. As long as the sides were equal, neither side could have control.

To keep this balance, Missouri was allowed to enter the United States as a slave state, and another territory, Maine, entered as a free state. In addition, Congress decided to draw an imaginary line across the country at the southern border of Missouri. As part of the Missouri Compromise of 1820, slavery would be forbidden in territories and states to the north of this line but permitted in Missouri and in those areas to the south of the line. This compromise kept the balance of power between the two sides. However, it also officially divided the nation in two sections, the North and the South.

The Missouri Compromise helped preserve peace in Congress until 1850, when once again new territories sought statehood. Again there was fear that the balance of power would be destroyed. To solve this problem, Congress passed several laws. The Compromise of 1850 was the name later given to these laws. One law allowed California to enter the country as a free state, but no slave state was added along with it. Instead, the idea of "popular sovereignty" developed. Popular sovereignty meant that the people living in the state or territory would decide for themselves whether slavery would be allowed. Thanks to some of the laws in the Compromise of 1850, the other western lands gained from Mexico would decide the slavery question for themselves.

The Southern congressmen were not yet content. The compromise so far did not keep the balance of power, because no slave state entered the Union to balance California. To settle this argument, Congress added another feature to the compromise: the Fugitive Slave Law. This law required all citizens throughout the United States to help return all runaway slaves to their masters. Even if slaves ran away to a Northern state where slavery was illegal, citizens were required to help capture them and send them back to the South.

Under the new law, any Northerner who helped slaves run away or who hid runaways would be punished. Such punishments varied. A jail sentence of six months might be imposed. Some whites received only fines, but others were whipped in public.

The Fugitive Slave Law satisfied the South, as all Northerners had to respect the Southerner's right to own slaves. However, it angered many Northerners. They believed that the South was forcing them to support the institution of slavery in their states. But Southerners contended that by not enforcing the Fugitive Slave Law, Northerners would be forcing them to accept antislavery beliefs.

In an attempt to balance the Fugitive Slave Law, Congress passed still another law. This law ended the buying and selling of slaves in the District of Columbia. Because of all these different laws, neither side was completely comfortable with the Compromise of 1850. The Compromise did not last long. Within a few years, both sides were angry. Northern politicians feared a takeover of the country by the Southern slave owners. Southerners, meanwhile, had their own ideas. They labeled some Northerners in the Republican party (founded in 1854) as "Black Republicans" because of their support of abolition, or the complete outlawing of slavery. These Southerners thought that Black Republicans wanted to free all the slaves in order to destroy the South.

Thousands of miles of new territory had been added to the nation, most of it won from Mexico. The question was, would these new lands enter the Union as slave states or free states?

In 1854, Illinois Senator Stephen Douglas came up with a new compromise, which he forced through Congress. According to this

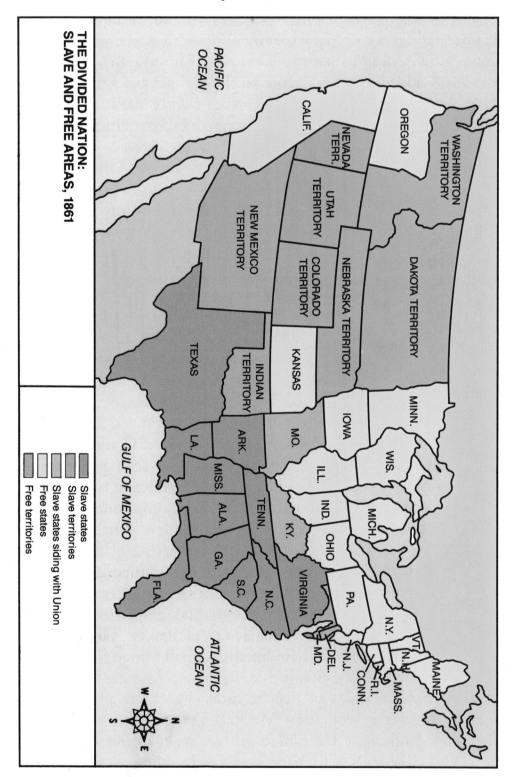

**THE DIVIDED NATION:
SLAVE AND FREE AREAS, 1861**

Slave states
Slave territories
Slave states siding with Union
Free states
Free territories

compromise, the new states would decide for themselves whether to allow slavery. On that October night in 1854, Senator Douglas proudly declared this plan to the audience in Springfield, Illinois.

One man heard the senator's words and did not like them one bit. He was a lanky, awkward-looking lawyer who had recently served in the House of Representatives. His name was Abraham Lincoln. Lincoln did not like the new compromise, which was called the Kansas-Nebraska Act, because it meant that slavery might be extended into Northern states, if the new Northern states wished. It meant that the vast lands in the central part of the country no longer had to follow the Missouri Compromise of 1820. The Kansas-Nebraska Act meant that slavery might be given a new life.

Abe Lincoln had retired from politics, but now he saw that he could not sit still and allow Senator Douglas to speak unchallenged. Two days later, at the State Fair, Lincoln addressed the crowd. He spelled out the danger of the Kansas-Nebraska Act, that slavery would grow instead of dying out.

"Wherever slavery is, it has been first introduced without law," he told the crowd. It would only make matters worse if a new law permitted the "monstrous injustice" of slavery into new states.

All across the country men and women were arguing the question. The battlefield was the new state of Kansas. Proslavery and antislavery forces fought in cities and towns throughout the state. The situation became so violent that this part of the frontier became known as "Bleeding Kansas."

In 1856 the fanatical abolitionist John Brown burned the city of Lawrence, Kansas, to the ground, killing slave owners and freeing slaves. This was but one example of the high emotions the slavery issue stirred up across the land. Southerners were outraged and claimed that wild-eyed Northerners were going to march south to free all the slaves. The two sections of the country were moving further apart.

6

ROCK BOTTOM

"You do not know how foresaken I feel here."

GRANT TO HIS WIFE

The decade of the 1850s, which was so difficult for the country, was also a hard one for Ulysses Grant. Although it began happily for him, it brought him mostly misery and failure.

On August 22, 1848, Ulysses S. Grant married Julia Dent in St. Louis, Missouri. The Mexican War had ended six months earlier, and Grant managed to get a two-month leave. After the wedding, the happy couple traveled to Ohio to stay with Grant's parents for a while. Then Grant was assigned to a regiment in Detroit, where he and Julia would live for the next two years. During that time their first child, Frederick Dent Grant, was born.

In the spring of 1852, the Fourth Infantry Regiment, Grant's regiment, was ordered to the Pacific coast. Julia was pregnant with their second child at the time. She could not make the long trip west. Grant had to go alone, and he quickly became homesick, missing his wife and his little son. He wrote to Julia: "I am almost crazy sometimes to see Fred."

Julia lived with her parents in St. Louis during this time. In July 1852, she gave birth to a second son, Ulysses S. Grant, Jr. Grant was stationed at Columbia Barracks at Fort Vancouver in the Oregon Territory, and later at Fort Humboldt in California. He disliked this lonely outpost and wrote to Julia, "You do not know how foresaken I feel here."

As the months wore on, his loneliness grew. He was unhappy that he did not make enough money to pay the cost of bringing his family out West. He began drinking to put the feelings of loneliness out of his mind. He did not drink a lot, but his body could not tolerate much alcohol. A small amount made him very drunk. He was so upset about being alone that he did not care what his drinking did to him. His appearance became sloppy. He did not shave for days, and he missed meals.

Lieutenant Colonel Robert Christie Buchanan, Grant's superior officer at Fort Humboldt, did not like Grant or his drinking. He made Grant's life even more miserable. Buchanan helped spread rumors about Grant's drinking. Whenever something went wrong at the fort, Buchanan blamed Grant.

Grant finally asked for a transfer to another military unit. He hoped that a new job in a different place would make him feel better. But his request was denied.

Finally, feeling hopeless, Grant decided to resign from the army. This was an extreme step, but Grant felt he had to do it. His life in the military had become unbearable.

Grant resigned from the army and traveled back to St. Louis. In October 1854, he and Julia were reunited after more than two years of separation. Grant was overjoyed to be with his wife and two sons. He hoped that his problems would now be over.

But returning to civilian life was not easy. In the military he had had a guaranteed job. But he did not have the kind of skills that were necessary to get a civilian job. Finally the Grants went to live with Julia's parents on their farm near St. Louis.

In 1855, Julia gave birth to their first daughter, Nellie. The family moved to Julia's brother's house on the family land. Grant tilled soil, planted crops, and hoed potatoes. Julia raised chickens and took care of the children. The next year, Grant built their own home, called Hardscrabble, on land that Julia's father had given them. For the time being, the family was happy.

More misfortune was soon to come. Grant was not able to make a living from the farm. The family needed another source of income. From the middle of 1856 through the beginning of 1857, Grant sold firewood on the streets of St. Louis. He hauled the wood into town and then stood sadly beside the pile. He wore his fading blue army coat and hoped that people would buy his wood. He was a desperate man.

Grant reached the point where he had to ask his father for money. He was humiliated. He was 35 years old and unable to support his wife and children. Jesse Grant was a stern man. He could not forgive his son for resigning his army post. He refused to help.

In 1858 the Grants lost their home, which was sold to pay off debts. Ulysses Grant became sick with despair. He developed ague, a sickness that causes chills, fevers, and sweating. He was penniless and sick, and he could see no hope for the future. He had hit rock bottom.

Julia Grant took over. She approached her cousin, Harry Boggs, who had a collection firm in St. Louis. His business was to collect late rents from people who did not pay their bills on time. Boggs gave Grant a job as a rent collector.

From the winter of 1858 to the summer of 1859, Grant worked for Boggs. He hated the job. He was still a shy man and could not be harsh with the poor people who were unable to pay their bills. Instead of trying to force money out of them, he felt sorry for them. Grant and Boggs argued, and Grant finally quit.

In August 1859, some of Grant's friends in St. Louis tried to get him a job as a county engineer. Grant ran for election to the post, but he did not receive enough votes.

By the end of 1859, Grant decided to ask his father again if he would help the family. Jesse Grant's heart softened. He offered his son a job in his leather goods store in Galena, Illinois. In the summer of 1860, Grant and Julia packed their belongings and headed for Galena. Hope returned to their lives. Grant would once again have a steady job and be able to support his family.

Life was better in Galena. Ulysses and Julia Grant got along with their neighbors. People were friendly, and life was calm. Working in the family store was not as awful as Grant thought it would be.

But life was about to change drastically for Ulysses Grant. On November 6, 1860, Abraham Lincoln was elected president. Lincoln was a Republican. During the campaign, Southerners had depicted him as an abolitionist, even though Lincoln had repeatedly said he did not support the destruction of slavery. But throughout the South he was known as a reformer who would bring to an end all of the South's fine old institutions.

With Lincoln's election, the split between the North and South became a crisis. Secession—the separation of states from the United States—was the Southern answer to the crisis. Many white Southerners saw secession in the same patriotic way that Americans had seen the revolution of 1776, when the 13 colonies broke away from Britain. These Southerners pictured themselves as fighting for independence. At the same time, they saw Abraham Lincoln as a present-day version of King George III.

Even before Lincoln took office in March 1861, seven Southern states left the Union and formed their own country, called the Confederate States of America. The states of South Carolina, Mississippi, Florida, Alabama, Georgia, Louisiana, and Texas agreed that joining the Confederacy was the only way to protect their rights. Jefferson Davis was chosen to be president of the new government.

After the Confederacy was formed, almost all the land within its borders that had been owned by the United States was taken over by the Confederate government. Fort Sumter in South Carolina was surrounded by Confederate troops. Its commander, Major Robert Anderson, told Washington that he was running out of supplies. The Confederate government would not allow President Lincoln to send supplies.

On April 12, 1861, Confederate general P. G. T. Beauregard told Major Anderson to surrender Fort Sumter because it was on Confederate land. Major Anderson refused to surrender. The Confederates opened fire. With these first shots, the fight between the North and the South reached a new, violent stage. The Civil War had begun. Within days, four more states—Virginia, Arkansas, Tennessee, and North Carolina—seceded from the United States and joined the Confederacy.

President Lincoln issued a call for troops. He asked for 75,000 volunteers to serve for 90 days. He hoped that the Southern uprising would be put down in that time.

Ulysses Grant heard the call. He realized that the nation was in great need of trained military men. He also felt he owed a debt to the government, which had paid for him to attend West Point. Besides that, his life outside the military had been disastrous. Almost every attempt at making a living had been a failure. He had been unable to support his family without the aid of others. He made the only choice he felt he could. He volunteered to join the army.

7

THE NORTHERN ARMY

"To work an army of five hundred thousand with machinery for a peace establishment of twelve thousand...is no easy task."

U.S. SECRETARY OF WAR EDWIN STANTON

Grant's first assignment was to help outfit and train companies in and around Galena, Illinois. He met with many important people of the area, including congressmen, lawyers, and businessmen. Congressman Elihu B. Washburne realized that the 39-year-old West Point graduate deserved a higher place in the wartime army. He used his political contacts to have Grant appointed a colonel in the Seventh District Regiment.

As colonel, Grant arranged to have a congressman address his troops to inspire them. At the end of his speech, the congressman introduced Grant. Grant, to his horror, found himself standing before an audience, expected to speak. He had always been shy, and it was no different now. He cleared his throat and said simply, "Men, go to your quarters!"

The next month, the disastrous Battle of Bull Run was fought. The Union military leaders realized the army needed more experienced officers in battle. In August, Grant received word that he had been appointed brigadier general. He was to take command of troops in southeastern Missouri and southern Illinois.

The army of which Grant now found himself a part was a peacetime army. The United States government had not expected to fight a war, especially against Americans. When the war broke out, the entire army was disorganized. There was no real chain of command. President Lincoln, as commander in chief, was officially in charge of the army, but he had very little understanding of military matters.

Unfortunately, the secretary of war had as little training in army matters as the president did. Army commanders took advantage of this. Each commander controlled his own unit and was his own boss. In the past, the situation had been different. During the Mexican War, Winfield Scott had had a tight grip on his units. There was no "supreme commander" during that war, but it was small compared with the scope of the Civil War.

The U.S. government had another huge problem. At the start of the war, most of the trained military men from the South left the federal army. Many soldiers, such as Robert E. Lee, did not want to stay in the Union if it meant fighting against their families and friends. Lee considered himself a Virginian first and an American second. In all, more than 80 percent of the federal army's officers who had originally come from the South returned to join the Confederacy. This left few officers for the Union.

President Lincoln had to replace these experienced officers, and quickly. If a senior military man asked the president for a post, he simply got one. The Union army was desperate. Lincoln appointed several "political generals" as well: men who received high military positions because of their political connections, and not because of any understanding of military matters. These men did not always work out.

There were also problems with the soldiers. The majority of Union soldiers were farmers and merchants who had received little or no training. Most people thought that the war would end very quickly. The government called for volunteers, and civilians answered, believing they would stay in the army for just three months.

The training of these first recruits was brief. Many officers believed that the key to victory was to put as many men as possible into the field. But training was vitally important, especially in the armies of that time. Men moved on the battlefield in large groups. They had to be well prepared in order to obey their commanders' orders. Without training, the divisions did not act together as an army. Instead, they scattered over the battlefields. The early battles of the Civil War were often scenes of complete confusion and panic.

The Union soldiers also went into battle without proper equipment. There was no standard uniform. Men wore whatever they liked. Some soldiers wore bright colors to show off. Some Union troops wore gray uniforms, but gray would later become the color of the Confederate uniform. After a few weeks, clothing became tattered, and the men looked like packs of homeless wanderers rather than crisp lines of soldiers.

Discipline was another problem. The volunteers were not used to the strict routine of army life. They disobeyed orders, fell out of step with their companies, and often got drunk. Many took to drinking when they had to stand for guard duty. Their commanders could not figure out how this happened. Eventually one officer noticed that when the men left for guard duty they carried their guns using both hands. This was very odd. The officer decided to inspect some guns. He learned that the men were going out to guard duty with their gun barrels filled with alcohol.

In many ways, the conditions were the same in the Confederate army. The Rebel soldiers were also civilians who had volunteered for service. They too believed that the war would end quickly, and they received little training. But the Confederate troops had more experience using guns. They were used to hunting and shooting game.

The matter of uniforms was confusing in the early stages of the war. Many men on both sides wore the same cadet gray, and their own men would sometimes shoot at them. After the Battle of Bull Run, the Northerners adopted a dark blue uniform, and the Southerners sported a uniform of cadet gray.

Once standard uniforms were agreed to, they appeared by the thousands. The sewing machine had recently been invented, and the Civil War gave this new device its first test. Seamstresses on both sides had churned out hundreds of thousands of uniforms of all types by the time the war came to an end. The idea of varied, standard clothing sizes was also introduced for the first time.

Perhaps the biggest difference between the two armies was in the arming of their men. Most firearms manufacturers were in the North, so the Union had a steady supply of pistols and rifles. The Confederacy had a hard time finding enough firearms to fight the war. The Confederate government arranged a deal with England to trade cotton for weapons.

Whereas the Rebel soldier often had little more than an old smoothbore musket or a Kentucky long rifle of relatively small caliber, the Yankee infantryman carried the Model 1861 Springfield rifle of .58 caliber—a barrel diameter of .58 inches. The Springfield was accurate at a distance of 300 yards. In the hands of an expert rifleman, it was still effective at more than 800 yards. The Springfield became the standard of the Union infantryman, and the federal government purchased more than one and a half million during the war.

Samuel Colt's firearms company supplied sidearms, or pistols, mainly to the Northern army. Colt's weapons were very reliable six-shooters. His Model 1860 revolver in .44 caliber made an ideal sidearm for the cavalryman and was sought by both sides during the war. In fact, Colt made no secret of the fact that, even though his factory was located in Hartford, Connecticut, he sold his weapons to whoever was willing to pay for them, Northerners or Southerners. Strictly a businessman, Colt referred to his arming of both sides as "my latest work on 'Moral Reform.'"

Many small-arms makers sprang up in the South during the war. They made copies of Colt's army and navy revolvers. However, none could equal the original Colt, nor could they make enough to keep up with the constant demand for weapons for the Confederacy.

One of the problems that most worried President Lincoln was the poor organization of the Union army. It was divided into too many separate units, with each unit on its own. There was little contact between the different armies. Lincoln knew he needed to have an experienced military officer in charge of planning and carrying out the war effort.

Congress created the position of general-in-chief of the army. The general-in-chief would have four assistants. One of these was the quartermaster general, who would make sure the troops received enough uniforms, shoes, tents, horses, and wagons. Another was the commissary general, who would be responsible for getting food supplies to the units. The third was the chief of ordnance, who would be in charge of fighting equipment. The fourth was the chief engineer, who had the job of making sure there were roads and bridges where the troops had to be moved. Once this structure was in place, the Union was on its way to becoming an organized outfit.

But most important of all was the appointment of a good leader as general-in-chief. The first man to hold the position was General Winfield Scott. Grant had served under Scott in the assault on Mexico City in the Mexican War. Scott was an able soldier, but he was 75 years old now and could hardly move about his office, let alone plan and carry out battles. In November 1861, he retired, and Lincoln chose George B. McClellan as his replacement.

Lincoln visited General McClellan (facing him, with moustache) and the Army of the Potomac on October 1, 1862

McClellan was a career military man and a leader of great intelligence. He had been appointed to West Point at age 15, one of the youngest students ever to attend the academy. Before his appointment, McClellan was in charge of the Army of the Potomac, the army that guarded Washington, D.C. His men were deeply devoted to him. McClellan was the only general in the army who could jump on a horse and get soldiers to leave their breakfasts and follow him.

McClellan took his appointment as general-in-chief very seriously. He spent months planning his war strategy. He trained troops very thoroughly and spent a great deal of time at it. In the meantime, other officers such as Grant were out in the field fighting. Within a short time, Lincoln began to worry that McClellan was moving too slowly. But McClellan had his own way of doing things, and he refused to be rushed.

As McClellan spent time planning, the Confederates were moving closer to Washington, D.C.. Confederate General Joseph Johnston set up his headquarters in Manassas, Virginia, only 30 miles from the Union capital. President Lincoln became alarmed. If McClellan did not act soon, the Confederates would take Washington.

8

ATTACK: FORT HENRY TO SHILOH

"The enemy is trying to escape and he must not
be permitted to do so."

GRANT AT FORT DONELSON

All this time, Ulysses Grant had been active in the West. He had learned a great deal about commanding a regiment and was learning more all the time. Still, most of his time had been spent drilling troops and protecting the countryside. He was itching for battle.

Grant's commander in the West was Major General Henry Halleck. Halleck, like McClellan, was extremely cautious. Grant saw that the two Confederate forts that guarded the Tennessee and Cumberland rivers might be taken with swift attack. Then Tennessee and Kentucky would be lost to the Confederates, and supply lines would be cut off.

Halleck turned Grant away the first time he asked permission to attack. He did not much like Ulysses Grant. Halleck had heard about Grant's "drinking problem" and did not quite trust him. Besides that, there were supply lines that had to be put into place before an attack could be begun.

Halleck also did not approve of the way Grant commanded his troops. He believed that a good leader was one who followed the rules of war that were written in army textbooks. He had even

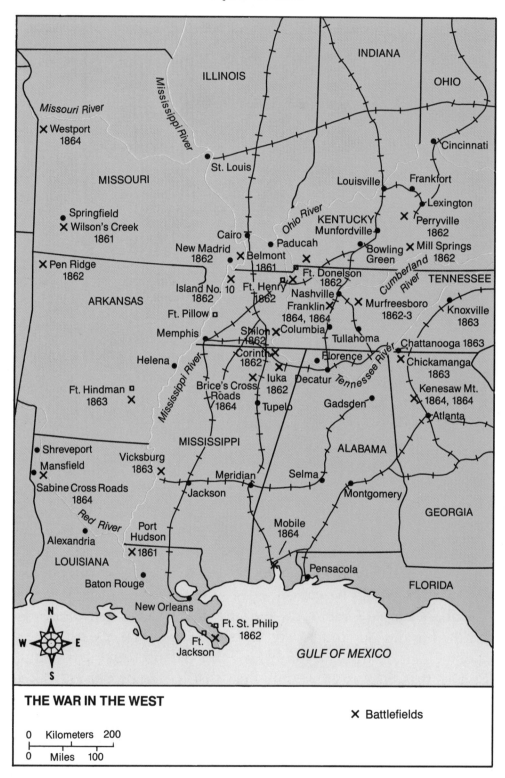

THE WAR IN THE WEST

✕ Battlefields

0   Kilometers   200

0   Miles   100

written a textbook of his own, called *Elements of Military Art and Science*. In his book, Halleck wrote that the best way to fight a war was by using the old ways of the great military leaders of Europe, especially Napoleon. This old style involved careful preparation and staying with the plans of battle no matter what happened.

Grant did not like this kind of plan. He felt that many opportunities came up during a battle that ought to be grasped. To Grant, a good commander had to be able to change his plans at any time. At West Point, he did not care to study military planning. He learned to take care of a problem as it happened.

Grant was determined to get around Halleck's decision. He sought out the help of another officer, flag officer Andrew Foote. Foote was in charge of gunboats in the area. Grant talked to him about his plan to take over the two Confederate forts. Foote liked the plan and wrote a letter to General Halleck telling him that he agreed with Grant. Foote's support helped Grant to get Halleck's permission to try the attack.

Finally, in January 1862, Grant got orders to "take and hold Fort Henry." This was what he had been waiting for. Quickly he moved 15,000 men up the Tennessee River. Also under his command was the Union fleet of gunboats under flag officer Foote. Foote and Grant planned a combined attack on the fort.

Grant looked for a place near the fort from which his men could attack. He planned the attack carefully. His infantrymen would storm the fort while the gunboats bombarded it with shells. But on the day of the attack, February 6, 1862, the army was not in place. Grant's troops were slowed down by bad roads. Foote's gunboats opened fire anyway, and the fort surrendered the same day. As it turned out, the rain had caused the river to flood the fort, and the Confederate soldiers inside were nearly drowning. So the victory at Fort Henry was surprisingly easy.

Next came the tougher job of capturing Fort Donelson. This was the first place where Grant showed his military genius. Once again, Grant planned a combined land and sea attack. This time, however, the gunboats were stopped after a brief attack. Grant's army had to win the fort alone. On February 16, 1862, the

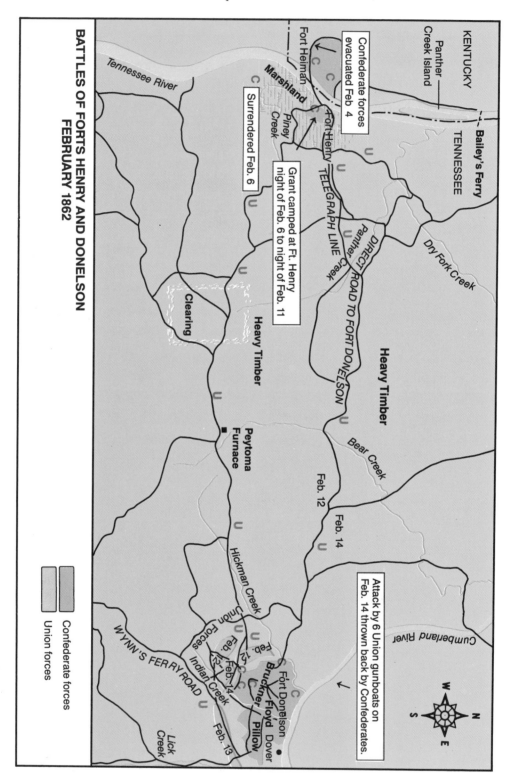

BATTLES OF FORTS HENRY AND DONELSON
FEBRUARY 1862

KENTUCKY

TENNESSEE

Panther
Creek Island

Bailey's Ferry

Tennessee River

Fort Heiman

Marshland

Piney Creek

Fort Henry

Confederate forces
evacuated Feb. 4

TELEGRAPH LINE

Panther Creek

Dry Fork Creek

DIRECT ROAD TO FORT DONELSON

Surrendered Feb. 6

Grant camped at Ft. Henry
night of Feb. 6 to night of Feb. 11

Clearing

Heavy Timber

Heavy Timber

Bear Creek

Feb. 12

Feb. 14

Peytoma
Furnace

Cumberland River

Attack by 6 Union gunboats on
Feb. 14 thrown back by Confederates.

N
W   E
S

Hickman Creek

Union Forces

WYNN'S FERRY ROAD

Indian Creek

Feb. 12

Feb. 14

Feb. 13

Lick Creek

Fort Donelson
Dover

Buckner
Floyd
Pillow

Confederate forces

Union forces

Confederate troops surrendered. This was the battle in which the Confederate general S. B. Buckner, who had once lent Grant money, asked for terms for surrender. "No terms except an unconditional and immediate surrender can be accepted," was Grant's reply. This statement quickly became famous throughout the North, and this was how President Lincoln first came to hear of Ulysses Grant.

Grant was promoted to major general after the victory at Fort Donelson. He quickly gained a reputation throughout the army for toughness and excellence.

Two months later, however, that reputation suffered. In April 1862, Grant's troops were camped at Pittsburg Landing on the Tennessee River, near a little church known as Shiloh Church. Grant was preparing to move the army and was trying to calculate the enemy's weakest point. At that moment, on April 6, the Confederate army attacked. Grant had not bothered to build protecting walls, and he had no men standing guard. The attack came as a complete surprise. Once again, Grant had to think fast or lose his entire army.

He quickly decided that no fancy plans would win the battle—only all-out fighting would. He ordered a full counterattack. The Union soldiers charged into the Rebel lines. Dozens fell dead. As one line of troops fell, Grant ordered the next line into the field. The men stepped over dead bodies to reach the enemy. The cries from the wounded filled the air. For two days the intense battle raged on.

The hottest fighting at the Battle of Shiloh, as it became known, was at the so-called Hornet's Next, at the center of the Union line. A young private named Leander Stillwell gave a particularly grim account of what he saw that day:

"I remember as we went up the slope and began firing, about the first thing that met my gaze was what out West we would call a "windrow" of dead men in blue; some doubled up face downward, others with their white faces upturned to the sky, brave boys who had been shot to death in 'holding the line.' Here we stayed until our last cartridge was shot away. We were then relieved by another

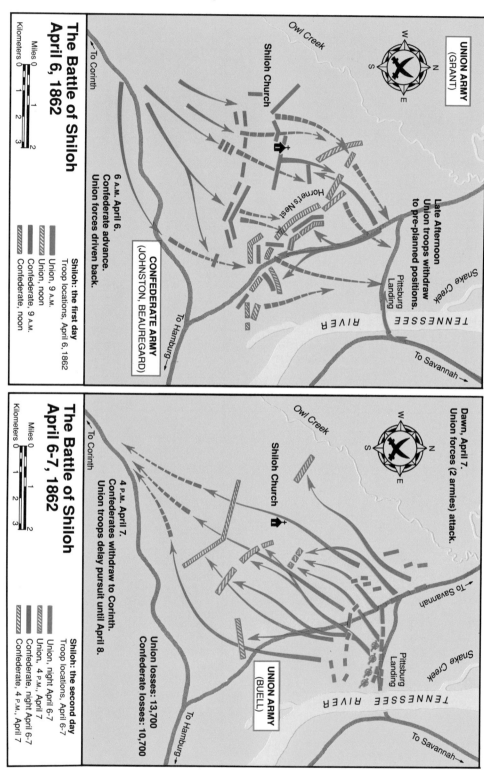

The Battle of Shiloh
April 6, 1862

Miles 0 | 1 | 2
Kilometers 0 | 1 | 2 | 3

Shiloh: the first day
Troop locations, April 6, 1862

Union, 9 A.M.
Union, noon
Confederate, 9 A.M.
Confederate, noon

6 A.M. April 6.
Confederate advance.
Union forces driven back.

CONFEDERATE ARMY
(JOHNSTON, BEAUREGARD)

UNION ARMY
(GRANT)

Late Afternoon
Union troops withdraw
to pre-planned positions.

Owl Creek
Shiloh Church
Hornet's Nest
Pittsburg Landing
Snake Creek
TENNESSEE RIVER

To Corinth
To Hamburg
To Savannah

W N S E

The Battle of Shiloh
April 6-7, 1862

Miles 0 | 1 | 2
Kilometers 0 | 1 | 2 | 3

Shiloh: the second day
Troop locations, April 6-7

Union, night April 6-7
Union, 4 P.M., April 7
Confederate, night April 6-7
Confederate, 4 P.M., April 7

4 P.M. April 7.
Confederates withdraw to Corinth.
Union troops delay pursuit until April 8.

UNION ARMY
(BUELL)

Dawn, April 7.
Union forces (2 armies) attack.

Union losses: 13,700
Confederate losses: 10,700

Owl Creek
Shiloh Church
Pittsburg Landing
Snake Creek
TENNESSEE RIVER

To Corinth
To Hamburg
To Savannah

W N S E

regiment. We filled our cartridge boxes again and went back to the support of our battery. The boys laid down and talked in low tones. Many of our comrades alive and well an hour ago, we had left dead on that bloody ridge. And still the battle raged. From right to left, everywhere, it was one never-ending, terrible roar, with no prospect of stopping."

Grant and his men did manage to stop the Confederates from winning the Battle of Shiloh, but the price was high. More than 3,000 men had been killed, including 1,754 Union soldiers. The battle was one of the bloodiest of the Civil War up to that time.

Halleck was furious with Grant's handling of the battle. For some time afterward, Grant was blamed for whatever went wrong with the army in the West. Grant's fine victories at Fort Henry and Fort Donelson were forgotten. Instead, Grant gained a new reputation. He was called the "Butcher of Men."

Grant would never forget Shiloh. In the past he had surprised other generals. Now they had surprised him. He had allowed his soldiers to go into battle unprepared. Grant felt so bad that he considered resigning from the army. His friend, General William T. Sherman, talked him out of it. Grant determined, however, that he would never make the same mistake again.

VICKSBURG

"Twenty thousand muskets and 150 cannon
belched forth death and destruction."

R.B. SCOTT, 67TH INDIANA VOLUNTEERS

t would not be easy for Grant to fix the damage to his reputation that Shiloh caused, but he was determined to do so. His big chance came seven months later at the Battle of Vicksburg.

Vicksburg, Mississippi, was another very important port for the South. Vicksburg was located on the Mississippi River, which was considered the dividing line between the East and the West. It connected western parts of the Confederacy with the rest of the South. Troops and supplies moved along the Mississippi. The location of many Southern forts on the river allowed the South to control the southernmost part of the river. Vicksburg was one such city.

In December 1862, Grant ordered General Sherman to attack Vicksburg. Sherman's men approached the city, which was located high up on a bluff. The Confederates fired down upon the invaders as they tried to climb the bluff, easily stopping them from reaching the city.

Flag officer David Farragut's ships took the key port of New Orleans in April 1861, and then pushed up the Mississippi River

Admiral David Farragut sealed off the southern Mississippi River, aiding Grant's attack on Vicksburg.

toward Vicksburg. Farragut's fleet sealed off the southern Mississippi from Confederate control.

Still, Grant realized that taking Vicksburg would be more difficult than he had thought. A more complicated plan was needed if the North was to capture the city. Grant decided to put together a new plan of attack. Sherman had faced major problems. The location of the city made it hard for the Union soldiers to reach. Also, the fact that the city was surrounded by rivers and swamps made it more difficult to attack. There was a great deal of rain in the winter, and the rivers flooded and the roads turned to mud. The Union troops could not hope to reach the city under such conditions.

Another problem was that Grant's men were in low spirits. "[A]t this time the North had become very discouraged with the war," Grant later wrote. "Many strong Union men believed that the war must prove a failure." This kind of thinking made victory even more difficult.

Grant, however, believed that things were not as hopeless as they seemed. The key to taking Vicksburg lay in securing a footing upon dry ground opposite the city.

In January 1863, the Union troops were stationed outside Vicksburg. The Mississippi was flooded, and rain continued to fall. No matter what plan Grant decided on, conditions were too bad for an attack to be carried out. Still, he had to keep his men busy. He designed two projects for them. For the first project, he ordered men to begin digging a canal next to the Mississippi River. When the Rebels saw the canal, they felt sure Grant's men would attack from there.

But then Grant ordered his men to clean up the mud from all the roads around their camp. Now the Rebels thought the Union troops would attack from land. In reality, Grant knew that both projects were useless. The canal and the road work were only meant to keep his men occupied. But they were also diversions to keep the enemy confused. The Confederates were not sure which way Grant would actually attack. Therefore, they had to divide their troops to defend against both kinds of attack. As the Confederates prepared their defense, Grant went to work making his real plans.

Many of the commanders in both armies had attended West Point and had studied the same military textbooks. They all had a similar way of planning and carrying out their battles. Ulysses S. Grant, however, was different. His plan for the attack on Vicksburg was unique, one that no other general would be able to guess.

The textbooks would have said there were two ways to attack Vicksburg: from the roads directly approaching the city, or from boats along the Mississippi River. The attackers would have to rely on orders being communicated from Washington, which was far off. And there would also have to be a supply line, a safe route through which the Union troops could get food and ammunition shipped to them.

Grant ignored all of this. He withdrew his messengers and stopped all communication with Washington, so that he was completely on his own in planning the battle. At Vicksburg he would practice his belief that a commander should rely on the conditions of the day in deciding his strategy.

He also did one other remarkable thing. He cut off the supply line and instead ordered his men to "live off the land." The troops were to carry enough supplies to last three days. After those supplies ran out, the men had to hunt and gather their own food. Whatever they needed that they could not find in the fields they were told to take from civilian homes. This daring plan gave the army more freedom. Troops could travel far from their home base without worrying about staying close to the supply line.

The Confederate commanders waited for Grant to attack. They were sure he would come either from the roads or from the river. They tried to outmaneuver the Union army by cutting off communication and supply lines. Of course, these attempts were useless since Grant had cut these lines.

Next Grant did the unexpected. Instead of attacking Vicksburg directly, he moved his army east and attacked the state capital, Jackson, Mississippi. Confederate General Johnston, who was waiting for the attack to come to Vicksburg, could not rally his men to defend the capital. The Union victory was swift.

From Jackson, Grant marched his men west, back toward Vicksburg. At Champion's Hill, Grant's army met the Confederates, and a terrible battle took place. But Grant remained calm. One soldier who fought on the hill later remembered Grant standing cool and calculating, smoking a cigar and ordering fresh assaults over the blood-covered ground. Grant's men won the battle and continued to push back toward Vicksburg.

After the Southern losses at Champion's Hill, the Confederate general John Pemberton had no way to get his army out of Vicksburg. Grant had divided his army, bringing some to Jackson and leaving others behind at Vicksburg. Pemberton now found himself surrounded, and Grant's assault began.

The fighting lasted for hours, with neither side able to claim victory. R. B. Scott, a Northern soldier with the 67th Indiana Volunteers, gave this account of the fierce fighting:

"Every experienced soldier...awaited the signal. It came, and in a moment the troops sprang forward, clenching their guns as they started on the charge....Twenty thousand muskets and 150 cannons belched forth death and destruction....Our ranks were now becoming decimated....The charge was a bloody failure."

The terrible number of injuries and deaths made clear to Grant that attacking the city directly was a serious mistake. Instead of fighting, he decided that siege warfare was the answer: It was best to surround the Confederates and wait. The city of Vicksburg was trapped. Eventually, the town would run out of supplies and food, and then they would have to surrender.

So the Union army waited. The seige lasted almost two months, but in the end, the city surrendered. Pemberton sent a note to Grant offering to surrender. On July 4, 1863, Grant accepted. The Battle of Vicksburg was over.

The news swept the country. The North was thrilled, the South was shocked. By taking Vicksburg, Grant had split the Confederacy in two. The enemy was weakened, and for the first time since the early days of the war, Northern victory looked like a real possibility.

The results were impressive, but Grant's methods were also much discussed. The usual way to win a battle was by direct attack. At Vicksburg, Grant had done something quite different. He had attacked other targets first, then laid seige to the city. The Confederates thought Vicksburg would never be taken, but Grant, using his unusual tactics, had done it. He accepted Pemberton's surrender the day after one of the other major events of the war, Lee's defeat at Gettysburg.

The Vicksburg campaign turned out to be Grant's masterpiece. The boldness of his strategy marked him as a military genius of the first order. Future students of wartime strategy would study Grant's capture of Vicksburg alongside the campaigns of that other military genius, Napoleon.

Grant Takes Charge

"Well, what kind of fellow is Grant?"

PRESIDENT ABRAHAM LINCOLN

For months, President Abraham Lincoln had been getting reports about Ulysses S. Grant, and most of them were not flattering. Lincoln once said, "Delegation after delegation has called on me with the same request, 'Recall Grant from command...'" Most of the reports concerned General Grant's drinking. Nobody liked the idea of a general who drank too much.

But President Lincoln had a different view of the matter. These stories of Grant's drinking could not be confirmed, and besides that, Grant was the only Union general who was winning battles. To one of the messengers who brought Lincoln news of Grant's drinking, the President barked, "If I knew what brand of whiskey he drinks I would send a barrel or so to some other generals."

In October, 1863, President Lincoln put Grant in command of all Union forces in the West. Shortly afterwards, on November 24 and 25, a great battle took place. The Army of the Potomac and the Army of the Tennessee joined forces against the Confederate army under General Braxton Bragg. It was to be a bitter struggle for control of the West.

Union armies under Grant's direction routed the Confederates at Missionary Ridge.

The Union armies were led by Major General George Thomas and Major General William Tecumseh Sherman, but Grant was in overall command. The armies came together at Missionary Ridge near Chattanooga, Tennessee. Grant drove his armies onward with tireless intensity, and in the end the Union forces won a major victory at the Battle of Chattanooga. The western states were now firmly in Union control.

Afterwards, President Lincoln met with Brigadier General John M. Thayer, who had served with Grant in the West. The president asked Thayer, "Well, what kind of a fellow is Grant?"

General Thayer said that Grant was one of the most brilliant generals he had ever served under. What's more, he told the president that the rumors about Grant's drinking were exaggerations. "I saw him repeatedly during the battles of Donelson and Shiloh on the field," said Thayer, "and if there were any sober men on the field, Grant was one of them."

In February 1864, Congress reinstated the army position of lieutenant general. This would be the highest rank in the army. Congress gave President Lincoln the authority to name a general in the Union army for the job. Lincoln had picked several commanders in the past, none of whom seemed to know how to win a war. By now he had heard enough about Grant. He had read the reports of Grant's victory at Fort Donelson, his brilliant campaign at Vicksburg, and his tireless work at Chattanooga. He chose Grant for the new position and sent word for him to return to Washington.

Grant left his post in the West and journeyed to Washington. With him was his son Fred, who was now 14 years old. By this time Grant's popularity had turned around. The North was tired of weak generals, and Grant's toughness had become widely known. Some newspapers even mentioned the possibility of Grant's running for president. Grant, however, said he was not interested in anything but fighting and winning the war.

When Grant arrived in Washington, he was greeted by cheering crowds. He shyly acknowledged the cheers and then dashed off to his hotel. Even here, however, he was in the spotlight. When he went to the hotel's restaurant for dinner, the room filled with whispers as people pointed out the general. Then a man stood up and cried, "Three cheers for Grant!" And the room rang with cheers. Again, the shy man simply nodded his thanks.

Shortly afterward, Grant had his meeting with the president. The general arrived at the White House dressed in an old, faded uniform. He chewed on the end of a cigar, and he walked with a slouch. He was not a noble, dignified man, but he was a winner. President Lincoln promoted him to lieutenant general and made him commander of all Union armies.

The president had complete faith in Grant. He trusted him more than any of the other generals who had led the Northern army. Grant had proved himself by winning battles, which was, after all, the job of a general. Lincoln did not even bother to ask Grant what his battle plans would be. He simply knew that Grant would defeat the Confederate army. Grant later said of the president, "All he wanted or had ever wanted was someone who would take responsibility and act."

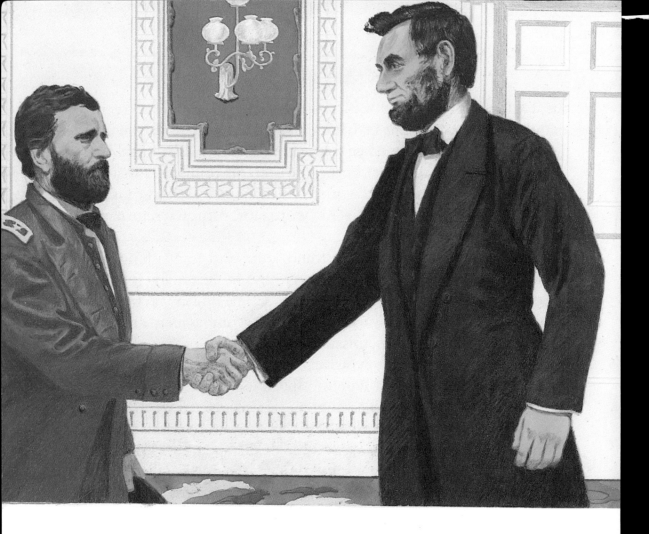

Grant accepted the new responsibility. Some people were critical of the sloppily dressed man from the West, but Grant did not care what was said about him. The most important thing for him was to be a good commander. According to Grant, it was not "the glitter and the drill and the show" that was important. Instead, "the result on the field of battle was about all that really mattered." That was precisely why President Lincoln had chosen him.

In his new position as head of the Union armies, Grant made sure that the results he got were better than good. He looked at warfare as if it were a game. He tried to figure out where the enemy troops were located, but once he did, he did not attack directly. Instead, he quickly slipped past them.

The key for Grant was surprise. By not doing the expected, he kept the Confederate generals guessing. While they were confused, Grant organized his attack. He did not come up on the enemy from the front. Instead he divided his troops into three groups and sent each one out on the attack. One group would attack the enemy from the right side. The other two would attack from the left and down the center.

Then, before the Confederates could get over the sudden attacks, Grant ordered lightning raids. Whole divisions of Union soldiers streamed across the Southern landscape, destroying railroad tracks and roads. The Confederate army would be beaten before it even knew what had happened, and its supply and transport lines would be cut.

The railroads were especially important to the Southern army. Confederate Commander Thomas J. "Stonewall" Jackson used railroads at the beginning of the war, in the famous Valley Campaign. His troops fought two separate divisions of the Union army at the same time by traveling back and fourth on the railroad! The Union generals had a hard time figuring out where Jackson and his men were. By destroying the railroad tracks and roads, Grant's army made life considerably more difficult for the Confederates.

Grant had a cold, mechanical view of war. He fought to win, and to win, he knew, he must destroy the enemy. Destruction was a vital part of Grant's strategy. He said that he wanted to "strike through the deep South" and "cut the Confederacy into smaller pieces." In between those pieces, he would place his army. Each piece would have to fight Grant's men on its own. Because the sections were small, they were weaker.

Grant's overall battle tactics were a matter of simple arithmetic. He knew that the way to win each battle was to kill more of the enemy than they killed of his men. He also knew that the North had a larger population than the South, and thus a larger army. If the Northern armies could kill more Confederates in each battle, they would win the war. It was as simple, and as horrible, as that.

Grant was much criticized for his cold view of war. His tactic was to send as many men into the field as quickly as possible. As a battle raged on, he would not concern himself with how many men died, as long as more of the enemy died. General Grant's battles

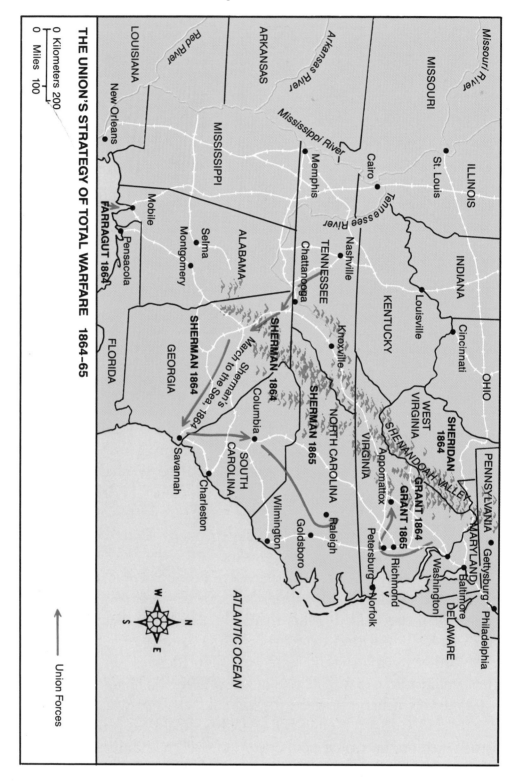

THE UNION'S STRATEGY OF TOTAL WARFARE   1864–65

were bloodbaths, and newspapers throughout the North cried out at the terrible loss of life.

Despite the heavy losses, as 1864 wore on the North saw that Grant's strategy was paying off. With each successful Union attack, the Confederate soldiers felt more and more discouraged. The feeling slowly grew in them that they could not win the war. The real purpose behind Grant's surprise attacks was to break the spirit of the Southern troops. This was necessary if the North were to win the war, and Grant was doing it.

With Grant in charge, the Northern army followed a single plan of operation for the first time. Grant might have stayed in Washington, to supervise all the complex operations that his plan involved, but that was not his style. Instead, when General George Meade brought the Army of the Potomac into the field to battle Robert E. Lee, Grant went with them. This was the first time the two great generals of the Civil War, Grant and Lee, would meet in battle.

In the campaigns of 1864–65, Grant enjoyed most of the advantages. He had almost twice as many troops as Lee and had no difficulty getting more troops when needed. He could mount attacks from other areas that would drain the Confederacy of soldiers, equipment, and, in the end, fighting spirit. He also had command of the seas and the assistance of the U.S. Navy. His armies were relatively well-fed, well-clothed, and well-equipped. All in all, Grant had the upper hand.

Lee had only the advantage of geography, and his own military genius. The land on which the two armies fought was good for defensive maneuvers. Lee knew this, and he took advantage of it. Also, he could depend on help from Richmond, the Confederate capital, and from General Beauregard, one of his best generals, on the James River.

But by 1864, death, disease, and desertion had reduced Lee's Army of Northern Virginia to a point well below its strength of earlier years. Also, the North had blockaded and captured Confederate arsenals. This had reduced the South's fighting power. Its soldiers were hungry, poorly dressed, and battle-weary. They knew

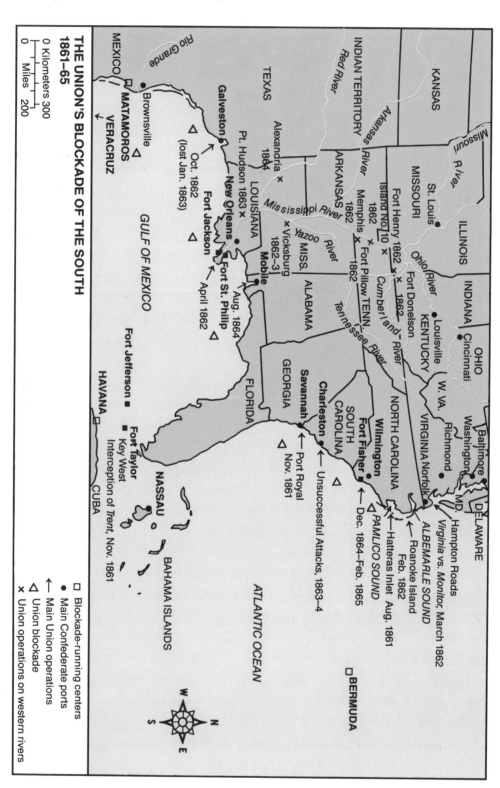

THE UNION'S BLOCKADE OF THE SOUTH
1861–65

0 Kilometers 300
0 Miles 200

□ Blockade-running centers
● Main Confederate ports
← Main Union operations
△ Union blockade
× Union operations on western rivers

that they could not count on more troops to help or replace them. They also knew that things were going badly almost everywhere in the Confederacy.

Still, Lee performed a miracle. For a year, he and his army fought off Grant's awesome attacks. His men were exhausted and ill-equipped, but they were devoted to their cause and their general. Lee himself proved to be one of the great military minds of all time.

The Wilderness Campaign was a long battle fought in a forest area in Virginia called the Wilderness. It lasted from May 4, when Grant crossed the Rapidan River in Virginia, until June 14, when he crossed the James River and began the siege of Petersburg. The details of this long and bloody conflict are confusing, but the general pattern is clear. Grant's objective was to destroy Lee's army and get to the Confederate capital of Richmond. Lee's job was to tangle Grant's troops in the Wilderness and destroy them. No single battle in his campaign reached the dimensions of Gettysburg or Shiloh, but as a whole it was the most costly campaign of the Civil War.

The Wilderness Campaign also saw some of the fiercest fighting of the war. Grant's total losses came to about 55,000. Lee's are unknown, but they were probably half that number.

Who won the Battle of the Wilderness? It is not an easy question to answer. On the face of it, the victory was Lee's. He kept Grant from breaking his lines and saved Richmond. He also caused terrible losses to Grant's army.

Yet Grant achieved most of what he had hoped for. He so punished Lee that the Army of Northern Virginia never really recovered. He thus prepared the way for a follow-up attack on Richmond from the south. He also ended his campaign with more men in his army than he had when he crossed the Rapidan.

In nearly every war in history, the story is told from the point of view of the generals who led the battles. But no matter which war you read about, whether it is the American Revolutionary War, the Civil War, or even the Trojan War in which the original Ulysses fought, it is the lone soldier who does the fighting. The common soldiers win battles that are credited to the generals. And the common soldiers have the best stories to tell about the real horror of war, the horror of killing another human being.

One such common soldier who fought in the Battle of the Wilderness was a young Union private named Warren Gross. On May 5, 1864, he found himself in the midst of some of the most terrible fighting of the war. He wrote:

"The scene of savage fighting with the ambushed enemy, which followed, defied description. No one could see the fight fifty feet from him. The roll and crackle of the musketry was something terrible, even to the veterans of many battles. The lines were very near each other, and from the dense underbrush and the tops of the trees came puffs of smoke, the 'ping' of the bullets, and the yell of the enemy. It was a blind and bloody hunt to the death, in bewildering thickets, rather than a battle.

"Amid the tangled, darkened woods, the 'ping! ping! ping!' the 'pop! pop! pop!' of the rifles, and the long roll and roar of musketry blending on our right and left, were terrible. In advancing it was next to impossible to preserve a distinct line, and we were constantly broken into small groups. The underbrush and briars scratched our faces, tore our clothing, and tripped our feet from under us, constantly.... Two, three, and four times we rushed upon the enemy, but were met by a murderous fire and with heavy loss from concealed enemies. As often as we rushed forward, we were compelled to get back.... The uproar of the battle continued through the twilight hours. It was eight o'clock before the deadly crackle of musketry died gradually away, and the sad shadows of night, like a pall, fell over the dead in these thickets. The groans and cries for water or for help from the wounded gave place to the sounds of the conflict...."

During this fighting, various campfires and cannon fire set off individual fires among the wooded areas. Soon both sides were fighting flames as well as each other. Private Gross briefly described the outcome: "During the conflict our men had exhausted their ammunition and had been obliged to gather cartridges from the dead and wounded. Their rifles, in many instances, became so hot by constant firing, that they were unable to hold them in their hands. The fire was the most terrible enemy our men met that day, and few survivors will forget this attack of the flames on their lines."

The Battle of Spotsylvania took place less than a week later (May 8–12). Disregarding losses, Grant tried to attack one side of Lee's troops at Spotsylvania Court House without success. Five bloody days of trench warfare followed. On May 11, Grant sent word to Halleck: "I propose to fight it out along this line if it takes all summer." The Union lost 12,000 men to death or injury as Lee fought off the Union blows. Heavy Confederate losses were never officially released.

Private Gross was not the only one who could tell some chilling stories about these battles. For instance, Robert Stiles, a young Confederate, described his experience at the end of the day on May 10. Dusk was approaching, and it seemed as though the fighting was over for the day.

"The troops supporting the two Napoleon guns of the Howitzers were, as I remember, the Seventh (or Eighth) of Georgia and the First Texas. Toward the close of the day everything seemed to have quieted down, in a sort of implied truce. There was absolutely no fire, either of musketry or cannon. Our weary, hungry infantry stacked arms and were cooking their mean and meager little rations. Someone rose up and, looking over the works—it was shading down a little toward the dark—cried out: 'Hello! What's this? Why, here come our men on a run, from—no, by Heavens! Its the Yankees!' and before anyone could realize the situation or even start toward the stacked muskets the Federal column broke over the little work between our troops and their arms, bayoneted or shot two or three who were asleep before they could even awake, and dashed upon the men crouched over their low fires—with cooking utensils instead of weapons in their hands. Of course they ran. What else could they do?" But the Confederate soldiers were quick to respond, and the Union attack was easily driven back. "When it became evident that the attack had failed, I suggested to the chaplain—who happened to be with the Howitzer guns, perhaps for a sundown prayer meeting—that there might be some demand for his ministrations where the enemy had broken over; so we walked up there and found their dead and dying piled higher than the works themselves. It was almost dark, but as we drew near we saw a wounded Federal soldier clutch the pantaloons of Captain Hunter, who at the moment was passing by, frying pan in hand, and heard him ask with intense eagerness: 'Can you pray, sir? Can you pray?'

"The old captain looked down at him with a peculiar expression, and pulled away, saying, 'No, my friend, I don't wish you any harm now, but praying's not exactly my trade.'"

If anything, the Confederates were impressed with the number of men who kept coming after them one after another. At times, it must have seemed as if Grant had brought in the entire Union army. Perhaps the words of one Confederate veteran of the Spotsylvania fight described best what Johnny Reb thought about Ulysses Grant: "We have met a man, this time," he wrote home, "who either does not know when he is whipped, or who cares not if he loses his whole Army."

At both the Wilderness and Spotsylvania, Lee had guessed what Grant would do and was able to outmaneuver him and successfully defend his positions. It is easy to imagine how frustrating this must have been for Grant. Once more he tried to outdo his onetime West Point classmate.

On June 3, 1864, at the Battle of Cold Harbor, Virginia, the Union Army lost 7,000 men in a few hours in a head-on assault. During this battle, Union soldiers pinned pieces of paper with their names and addresses on their backs. They were certain that they would be shot down as they charged at the Confederates, and they wanted to make sure their bodies would be recognized.

Grant's men had been in almost constant battle for nearly a month now. Knowing how many of their friends and comrades had died did not help the matter any. But they went on, for they were soldiers, and it is a soldier's duty to follow orders.

The Confederates were no better off. One Confederate, Colonel William Oates, described the bloodshed at Cold Harbor on June 3, 1864:

"As Captain Noah B. Feagin and his skirmishers crawled over the works I thought of my piece of artillery. I called out: 'Sergeant, give them double charges of canister; fire, men; fire!' The order was obeyed with promptness. The enemy were within thirty steps. They halted and began to dodge, lie down. They halted and began to dodge, lie down, and recoil. The fire was terrific from my regiment, the Fourth Alabama on my right, and the Thirteenth Mississippi on my left while the piece of artillery was fired more rapidly and better handled than I ever saw one before or since. The blaze of fire from it at each shot went right into the ranks of our assailants and made frightful gaps through the dense mass of men. They endured it but for one or two minutes, when they retreated, leaving the ground covered with their dead and dying. There were three men in my regiment killed, five wounded. My piece of artillery kept up a lively fire on the enemy where they halted in the woods, with shrapnel shell.... Sharp-shooting was resumed. The stench from the dead between our lines was sickening. It was so nauseating that it was almost unendurable; but we had the advantage, as the wind carried it away from us to them. The dead covered more than five acres of ground about as thickly as they could have laid."

Contrary to what some Confederates must have believed, Grant was not a cold-blooded murderer. He just felt that it was better to kill many enemy soldiers in a few battles. To kill a few soldiers here and there would lead to many more battles. More men would die in the long run. In Grant's view, he was saving lives by using this strategy.

After three battles with no clear winners—at the Wilderness, Spotsylvania, and Cold Harbor—Grant decided to move his army south of the James River to Petersburg, which was located 20 miles below Richmond. Petersburg was thought of as the "back door to Richmond." Grant, in other words, would approach the Confederate capital from the rear. His intention in doing this was to cut

Grant posed for the camera in front of his tent during the long siege of Petersburg.

off transportation connections with the South. However, the Union commander, William F. Smith, made mistakes in the battle and prevented Grant from taking Petersburg. The city withstood four days of battering, and another 8,000 Union soldiers were killed or wounded. When this attack failed, Grant decided that it was time to lay siege to Petersburg until the Confederates surrendered. The Siege of Petersburg would take nine months and would end with Lee's surrender at Appomattox. It would also be the longest siege of the war.

THE BEGINNING OF THE END

"I mean to end the business here."

GENERAL ULYSSES S. GRANT

Commander Grant could not concern himself merely with the battles in which he fought. As leader of the Union armies, he also had to think about what the other generals were doing. To him, each battle was as important as the entire war.

When Grant took control of the Union army, he coordinated the movements of its units. This enabled him to use the full power of his forces. Grant was a general who realized the importance of manpower. The best way to crush the enemy, he often said, was by attacking him straight. Grant wanted more than one unit at a time in battle. There was strength in numbers.

For Grant, it was not enough that the troops under his command did well. The other generals—Banks and Sherman, for example—had a job to do, and each had to carry out his responsibilities if the Union was to be victorious. Everyone, from the lowest private to the highest-ranking general, had to take part in the war effort.

It was with this in mind that General William Tecumseh Sherman began his famous "March to the Sea," which lasted from November 15 to December 21, 1864. General Sherman, however, had some ideas about how to fight the war that were different from

General William Tecumseh Sherman paused only briefly (here, at Atlanta) during his crushing March to the Sea.

Grant's. Grant believed the war would be won by defeating the enemy armies. Sherman thought that he could crush the spirit of the South. He marched his army of 60,000 men across Georgia to the Atlantic Ocean, wrecking the countryside. Sherman's march was one of the most brutal operations of the entire war.

The final campaign of 1864 was one of the most decisive. It deprived Robert E. Lee's army of its major source of supply and cut it off from the West. The Valley Campaign of 1864, as it would be called, was led by General Jubal Early as the Southern commander and General Phil Sheridan as the Northern commander. Although Grant was the overall commander, he was not present at this campaign, since it took place at approximately the same time as the Wilderness Campaign, further to the east.

Like all wars, the Civil War was filled with some rather strange events. And, as in all wars, the boys and young men who were put on the firing line soon became used to the fear and gunfire of battle. In this particular campaign, the young cadets at the Virginia Military Institute (VMI) at Lexington had their first experience of war at a place called New Market. John Wise, then a cadet of 17, remembered the excitement of the day when they were told they would be going into combat against a Union force. Like many older men, he remembered it as "the most glorious day" of his life. It was a gloomy, overcast Sunday morning when Wise and his fellow cadets reached New Market. A six-gun battery of Southern artillery waited in a graveyard outside a church to support them. It was 11 o'clock on May 10, 1864, when everyone was in position and the enemy was in plain sight.

"My orders were to remain in the wagons at the bend in the pike, unless our forces were driven back; in which case we were to retire to a point of safety. When it became evident that a battle was imminent, a single thought took possession of me, and that was, that I would never be able to look my father in the face again if I sat on a baggage-wagon while my command was in its first, perhaps its only, engagement. He was a grim old father, at the moment commanding at Petersburg.... If, now that I had the opportunity, I should fail to take part in the fight I knew what was in store for me. Napoleon in Egypt had pointed to the Pyramids and told his soldiers that from their heights forty centuries looked down upon them. My oration, delivered from the baggage-wagon, was not so elevated in tone, but equally emphatic. It ran about this wise:

'Boys, the enemy is in our front. Our command is about to go into action. I like fighting no better than anybody else. But I have an enemy in my rear as dreadful as any before us. If I return home and tell my father that I was on the baggage guard when my comrades were fighting I know my fate. He will kill me with worse than bullets—ridicule. I shall join the command forthwith. Anyone who chooses to remain may do so.'

"All the guard followed. The wagon was left in charge of the driver. Of the four who thus went, one was killed and two were wounded....

"Moving at double-quick we were in an instant in line of battle, our right near the turnpike. Rising ground in our immediate front concealed us from the enemy. The command was given to strip for action. Knapsacks, blankets, everything but guns, canteens and cartridge-boxes, were thrown down upon the ground. Our boys were silent then. Every lip was tightly drawn; every cheek pale; but not with fear. With a peculiar nervous jerk we pulled our cartridge-boxes round to the front and tightened our belts. Whistling rifled-shell screamed over us as, ripping the hill-crest in our own front, they bounded over our heads. Across the pike to our right, Patton's brigade was lying down, abreast of us....

"Brave Evans, standing over six feet two, unfurled our colors that for days had hung limp and bedraggled about the staff, and every cadet in the Institute leaped forward, dressing to the ensign, elate and thrilling with the consciousness that 'This is War!'...

"Down the green slope we went answering the wild cry of our comrades as their musketry rattled out its opening volleys. In another moment we should expect a pelting rain of lead from the blue line crouching behind the stone wall at the lane. Then came a sound more stunning than thunder, that burst directly in my face; lightning leaped; fire flashed; the earth rocked; the sky whirled round, and I stumbled. My gun pitched forward, and I fell upon my knees....

"I knew no more. When consciousness returned it was raining in torrents. I was lying on the ground, which all about was torn and plowed with shell which were still screeching in the air and bounding on the earth....

"Bloody work had been done. The space between the enemy's old and new positions was dotted with their dead and wounded—shot as they fled across the open field. But this same exposed

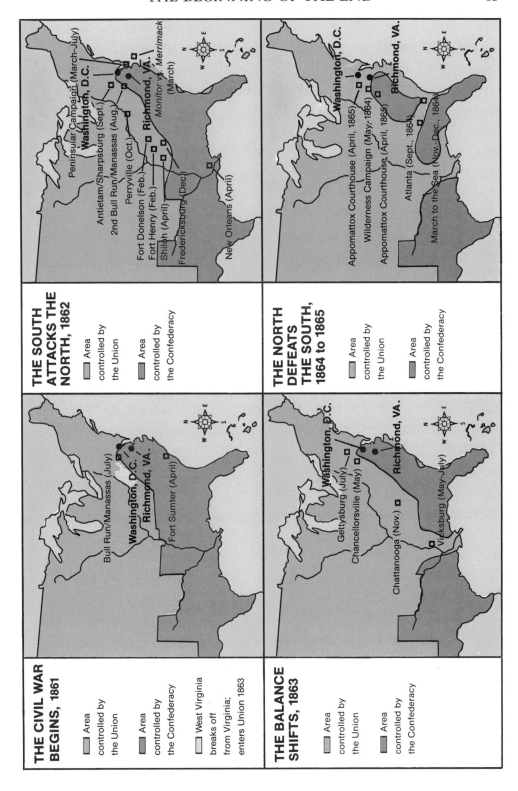

THE SOUTH ATTACKS THE NORTH, 1862

Peninsular Campaign (March–July)
Washington, D.C.
Antietam/Sharpsburg (Sept.)
2nd Bull Run/Manassas (Aug.)
Perryville (Oct.)
Richmond, VA.
Monitor vs. Merrimack (March)
Fort Donelson (Feb.)
Fort Henry (Feb.)
Shiloh (April)
Fredericksburg (Dec.)
New Orleans (April)

■ Area controlled by the Union
■ Area controlled by the Confederacy

THE NORTH DEFEATS THE SOUTH, 1864 to 1865

Washington, D.C.
Richmond, VA.
Appomattox Courthouse (April, 1865)
Wilderness Campaign (May–1864)
Appomattox Courthouse (April, 1865)
Atlanta (Sept., 1864)
March to the Sea (Nov.–Dec., 1864)

■ Area controlled by the Union
■ Area controlled by the Confederacy

THE CIVIL WAR BEGINS, 1861

Bull Run/Manassas (July)
Washington, D.C.
Richmond, VA.
Fort Sumter (April)

■ Area controlled by the Union
■ Area controlled by the Confederacy
□ West Virginia breaks off from Virginia; enters Union 1863

THE BALANCE SHIFTS, 1863

Washington, D.C.
Gettysburg (July)
Chancellorsville (May)
Richmond, VA.
Chattanooga (Nov.)
Vicksburg (May–July)

■ Area controlled by the Union
■ Area controlled by the Confederacy

ground now lay before, and must be crossed by our own men, under a galling fire from a strong and protected position. The distance was not three hundred yards, but the ground to be traversed was a level green field of young wheat. Again the advance was ordered. Our men responded with a cheer. Poor fellows! They had already been put upon their mettle in two assaults. Exhausted, wet to their skin, muddied to their eyebrows with the stiff clay through which they had pulled,—some of them actually shoeless after their struggle across the plowed ground,—they nevertheless advanced with great grit and eagerness; for the shouting on their right meant victory. But the foe in our front was far from conquered. As our fellows came on with a dash the enemy stood his ground most courageously. That batttery, now charged with canister and shrapnel, opened upon the cadets with a murderous hail the moment they uncovered. The infantry lying behind fence-rails piled upon the ground, poured in a steady, deadly fire....

"The men were falling left and right. The veterans on the right of the cadets seemed to waver. Ship, our commandant, fell wounded. For the first time the cadets seemed irresolute. Someone cried out, 'Lie down,' and all obeyed, firing from the knee—all but Evans, the ensign, who was standing bolt upright. Poor Stanard's limbs were torn asunder and he lay there bleeding to death. Someone cried out 'Fall back, and rally on Edgar's battalion.' Several boys moved as if to obey; but Pizzini, orderly of 'B' Company, with his Italian blood at the boiling-point, cocked his gun and swore he would shoot the first man who ran. Preston, brave and inspiring, with a smile lay down upon his only arm, remarking that he would at least save that. Collona, captain of 'D', was speaking words of encouragement and bidding the boys shoot close. The boys were being shot to pieces; manifestly they must charge or retire; and charge it was.

"For that moment, Henry A. Wise, our first captain...sprung to his feet, shouted the charge, and led the Cadet Corps forward to the guns. The guns of the battery were served superbly; the musketry fairly rolled. The cadets reached the firm greensward of the farmyard in which the battery was planted. The Federal infantry began to break and run behind the buildings. Before the order to 'Limber up' could be obeyed our boys disabled the trails and were close upon the guns; the gunners dropped their sponges and sought safety in flight. Lieutenant Hanna hammered a burly gunner over the head with his cadet sword. Winder Garrett outran another and attacked him with his bayonet. The boys leaped on the guns, and the battery was theirs; while Evans was wildly waving the cadet colors from the top of the caisson....

"We had a won a victory—not a Manassas...but, for all that, a right comforting bit of news went up the pike that night to General Lee; for from where he lay, locked in the death grapple with Grant in the Wilderness, his thoughts were, doubtless, ever turning wearily and anxiously towards this flank movement in the valley."

If there is one thing a soldier will always remember, it is the first experience of combat. What is important to remember is that fighting the people of another nation is one thing; fighting your own countrymen, as happened in the Civil War, is quite another. For many of the soldiers in that war it was a strange and disquieting experience to be at war with their own people. With that in mind, it should be obvious why John Wise would remember in minute detail that day at New Market.

In the early spring of 1865, Grant once again put his philosophy into action. He ordered General Sheridan to begin an attack against the Confederates. Sheridan headed for Five Forks, Virginia. Grant also sent Commander Warren as backup for Sheridan. The idea was that the Confederates would have less of a chance of stopping an attack that was led by two good leaders.

Warren's troops attacked at Five Forks from the enemy's side. Sheridan's men went at them head-on. Although Warren's troops began to slow down, Sheridan's did not. Sheridan rode on horseback in between his men as they fought. He hit them and yelled at them. "Move faster and hit harder," he commanded. The men felt his fury. The end of the battle brought a huge Northern success. According to Sheridan, "Half of the Southern troops ran to the Northern Army to surrender. The other half ran away in the retreat." Coordination of the Union army units had been the key.

LINCOLN'S GENERALS

President Lincoln struggled mightily to find the right man to lead his armies to victory. When the Civil War broke out, General Winfield Scott was in overall command. Scott's distinguished service went all the way back to the War of 1812. He had brilliantly led the nation's army in the Mexican War of 1846-48. Now, however, he was old and feeble. Nevertheless, he suggested the strategy that finally won the war. The so-called "Anaconda Plan" was designed to blockade Southern ports and strangle the Confederacy the way an anaconda snake strangles its prey. General George B. McClellan led the Union armies from November 1861 to July 1862. He had a great textbook understanding of warfare, but did not possess the boldness necessary to win battles. Finally, in March 1864, Lincoln found a man with the right combination of guts, energy, and daring: Ulysses S. Grant.

General Winfield Scott (seated), hero of the Mexican War, was the Union army's first commander.

General McClellan was nicknamed "Young Napoleon" after the brilliant French military leader.

The grizzled, determined Ulysses S. Grant was the perfect man to bring the Union to victory.

It was not long before the Confederacy felt the full effects of the Union army success. It was then that it began to fall apart. Grant's strategy was working. The Union hit at the Confederacy with enormous force, and the South had trouble holding up in battle. They simply did not have enough men to stop the North.

There were other problems, too. Transporting soldiers to battle was not always possible. Grant's men had done their job well. They had destroyed a large part of the South's railroad tracks. The remaining Southern routes were not well-built. The comparatively few soldiers that the Confederacy had could not always make it to the fight. And those that did make it to battle often did not have enough supplies. It was difficult to move supplies to many of the army units from Richmond, where the government was located, and from the units' command headquarters. Grant's army had isolated the units and cut their supply source.

Those Confederate units that did remain connected to headquarters still could not get enough supplies. The materials needed to make guns and cannon balls were not available. Southern troops went to civilian homes, asking for donations of metals. Women gave away their families' flatware, pots, and jewelry, which were melted down and used as the metal for war materials. The longer the war lasted, the harder it became for the South to produce war materials.

In addition, the Union navy had blockaded the South. The idea of a blockade began in the late summer and fall of 1862. Under Benjamin F. Butler, Union naval forces seized the tip of the peninsula between the James and the York rivers. Once this section of the blockade was completed, Union ships moved on to Hatteras Inlet, on the Outer Banks of North Carolina. By the middle of 1863–64, the Union blockade of Southern waterways was effective. Foreign and Confederate ships were prevented from traveling to and from Southern ports. These ships carried items that the South needed to fight the war. Thus, the South did not get sufficient supplies of war material or food staples from France and England, with whom they traded heavily early in the war.

As more and more battles were lost, pressure grew on the Confederate government to do something. Fear of losing the war spread. Members of the Confederate government constantly argued. They could not make decisions as easily as they had at the beginning of the war. They could no longer agree on what course of action to take.

Near the end of the war, morale was low throughout the South. Hope of winning the war disappeared. The great victory which the South had planned was nowhere in sight. The Northern armies continued to dominate the Confederacy, winning battle after battle. The South was slowly but surely being exhausted of both manpower and supplies.

At the beginning of 1865, with the situation growing worse for the South, hopes of the Southern people turned to one man— Robert E. Lee.

THE SOUTH SURRENDERS

"There is nothing left me to do but to go and see General Grant, and I would rather die a thousand deaths."

GENERAL ROBERT E. LEE

By the spring of 1865, Grant's strategy for destroying the Confederate army had all but succeeded. The Union army had two soldiers for every one Rebel. The South's supply lines were cut, and communication between Confederate armies was slow or nonexistent. It seemed only a matter of time before the South would be forced to surrender.

But the South still had General Robert E. Lee. Lee was regarded as the most brilliant general in America. President Lincoln had offered him command of the Union armies when the Civil War broke out, but Lee had made the painful decision to leave the army he had served for many years and join the Confederacy. Throughout 1864, Lee had shown his brilliance many times by outfoxing Grant in the Wilderness Campaign.

But the problems Lee faced were large. By March of 1865, he and his men were quartered at Amelia Court House, near Petersburg, Virginia. Their food and supplies were almost gone. Much of the Confederacy had been lost, thanks to Grant's idea of total war. Union soldiers under the command of General Sheridan were now coming after Lee. He had no choice but to try to slip away.

Lee ordered his men to set out for the Appomattox River. Crossing the river was his only means of escape. The army began the march in the middle of the night so that they would not be noticed.

The Confederate escape might have worked if it were not for General Grant. Grant's military experience told him that Lee would see the hopeless situation and try a bold escape. Grant therefore marched his men all night from Jettersville, Virginia, hoping to catch up with Lee.

Grant's army chased Lee into a pocket, with Generals Sheridan and Meade also closing in. On April 6, Meade's troops met the Rebel rear at Sayler's Creek. Heavy fighting took place. Grant had ordered his generals to use every available man, sending infantry, gunners, and cavalry out against the Rebels.

The Battle at Sayler's Creek started in the afternoon and went on well into the evening. As darkness descended, Lee could see that his losses were very heavy. Six thousand Confederate soldiers were captured. Lee had watched the encounter from a nearby hilltop. As night came on, he turned to one of his officers and said sadly, "General, that half of our army is destroyed."

But still Lee did not give up. He continued to push his men towards the Appomattox River. Grant counted on Lee doing just that. To stop Lee, he ordered Sheridan and Meade to attack at the same time. Their troops would come at Lee from the left and right, while Grant's would attack from the center.

The Confederates managed to get to the river. About half of Lee's men made it across. They burned down the bridge after them. This was supposed to stop the Union troops from coming after them, but in fact it trapped the Southerners.

Grant had once again planned a surprise attack. Sheridan's men were directly behind Lee's men. It was relatively easy for Grant to surround Lee's army. His men moved faster than at any time during the war. As Grant later wrote, he knew that the Union forces had "begun to see the end of what they had been fighting four years for.

In this painting, Sherman, Grant, Lincoln, and Admiral David Dixon Porter discuss the war's end.

Nothing made them tired. They were ready to move without food and travel without rest until the end." The end was near, and the Union soldiers could feel it.

The day before, after the attack at Sayler's Creek, General Sheridan reported to Grant his opinion: "If the thing is pressed I think that Lee will surrender." Grant decided it was time to press. On April 7, 1865, Grant wrote Lee a letter. In the letter he stated that it was hopeless for Lee's Army of Northern Virginia to continue to struggle. The war was over. Lee should surrender to save the lives of his men. Any more bloodshed would be Lee's responsibility if he did not put down his weapons.

Lee answered Grant's letter that same evening. He asked Grant what the terms of surrender would be. Grant replied the next day.

Peace was Grant's greatest wish. To end the war, Grant had only one demand to make. All of Lee's soldiers and officers must lay down their weapons and agree not to take up arms against the government of the United States.

The fighting between Lee's and Grant's troops stopped on April 9. That morning, General Lee said sadly to his bedraggled troops, "There is nothing left me to do but to go and see General Grant, and I would rather die a thousand deaths." But he sent Grant a note asking for a meeting.

The two generals met at a private home in the little town of Appomattox Court House. When Grant arrived, Lee was already there. Grant had not bothered to change his clothes and was wearing a dirty, torn private's uniform with a lieutenant general's stripes sewn on the shoulders. Lee, a Southern gentleman, wore his fanciest dress uniform, complete with sword. With his flowing grey hair and beard, he looked like a king. Grant, the victor, looked more like a badly beaten soldier.

Way back in his West Point days, Grant had shied away from the aristocratic boys from wealthy families who dressed and acted so formally. Grant had always felt inferior to them. Lee was one of those boys of noble bearing. Now, decades later, these two men, representing different types of Americans, faced one another at the end of the Civil War. Grant had never gotten over his shyness or feeling of inferiority, but he had learned how to fight a punishing war. That ability had led to this meeting.

The two men shook hands and then sat down to talk.

It was a solemn moment. They had served together in the old United States Army under General Winfield Scott. They had fought together in the Mexican War, where Lee had held a higher rank. Grant was painfully aware of how difficult this surrender must be for a proud man like Lee. He therefore began by talking about the old times. He said that he remembered Lee from Mexico. Lee nodded, shared a few words about the past, and then said politely, "I suppose, General Grant, that the object of our present meeting is fully understood. I asked to see you to ascertain upon what terms you would receive the surrender of my army."

Grant repeated the terms he had offered before. He requested only that Lee's men put down their weapons and not fight against the United States government. Then they wrote the terms out on paper and signed it.

Before Lee left, he told Grant that his men were very hungry. They had gone for some time on very little food. "I have, indeed, nothing for my own men," he said.

Grant ordered that 25,000 rations be sent to Lee's army. He then asked if there was anything else he could do.

Lee said there was one other thing. He would be grateful if Grant would allow his men to keep their horses.

Grant said, "I take it that most of the men in the ranks are small farmers, and as the country has been so raided by the two armies, it is doubtful whether they will be able to put in a crop to carry themselves and their families through the next winter without the aid of the horses they are now riding." He signed an order allowing the Confederate troops to keep their horses.

Lee thanked him. "This will have the best possible effect upon the men," he said. "It will be very gratifying and will do much toward conciliating our people."

The two men shook hands and went their separate ways.

Grant felt sad after the meeting. The end of the war was a great triumph for the North and for Grant. In a span of four years he had risen from a failed military man working as a clerk in his father's store to the commander who won the war. But it had been a long and difficult struggle. The entire country had suffered overwhelming tragedy, especially the South. Grant was sorry that so much destruction had taken place.

After the meeting, the officers of both armies got together at a private home. They socialized and toasted to the end of suffering. They acted as if they had been friends fighting battles under the same flag who had been separated for a long while. It seemed as if they had forgotten that they had, in fact, been fighting against one another. All these men had a great deal of respect for one another.

Once Lee surrendered, the war was all but over. A few generals had not heard of Lee's defeat. Confederate General Joseph Johnston

Robert E. Lee posed for photographer Mathew Brady at his home in Richmond at the war's end.

and Union General William Sherman continued to fight, but it was not long before they heard the news of Lee's surrender and laid down their arms.

On April 14, 1865, Major General Robert Anderson hoisted the Union flag over Fort Sumter, South Carolina, the site of the first battle of the war, and the first Confederate victory.

Grant knew that the war had been costly for both sides, both in blood and in money, but he believed the victory made the heavy price worth paying.

It is said that the winners write the history books. It should be noted that men on both sides fought bravely. The Confederacy was not beaten so much as exhausted of men, supplies, food, and munitions. It is hard for a man who is hungry and exhausted to fight at the peak of his performance. Still, many a Rebel soldier was willing to fight under impossible conditions. Grant had the compassion and decency to respect such men, who were once his enemy and were now his countrymen.

The Civil War ended in April 1865. It had lasted four long years. Many bloody battles had been fought. Untold destruction had taken place. Finally, the horror was over. Relief and jubilation swept the North. And nobody was more relieved than General Ulysses S. Grant.

13

GRANT ENTERS POLITICS

"It is not to be expected that such a rebellion as was fought between the sections from 1861 to 1865 could terminate without leaving many serious apprehensions in the mind of the people as to what should be done."

ULYSSES S. GRANT

Immediately after the surrender, Grant left Virginia. He headed for Washington, where he would bring the good news of the South's surrender to President Lincoln himself.

In Washington, Grant met with the president and took care of chores that were necessary to put an official end to the war. He communicated with all of his commanders, giving them official word of the end of the war. Plans were made to capture the few remaining Southern troops that had not heard of Lee's surrender. Grant also had to make arrangements to release the Confederate prisoners of war.

Grant completed all of this work within a few days. Now he had some time to spend with his wife. Mrs. Grant had come to Washington with him, but the children were attending school in New Jersey. On April 14, President and Mrs. Lincoln invited Grant and his wife to accompany them to the theater. Grant had told the president that he would go, though he probably did not want to. Formal social occasions always made him feel uncomfortable. But Mrs. Grant did not like the idea. She did not get along with Mrs.

Union troops paraded triumphantly through Washington, D.C., at the end of the war.

Lincoln. She insisted that the Grants visit their children instead of going to the theater. Grant sent word to the President and Mrs. Lincoln that he and Mrs. Grant would be unable to accompany them.

That afternoon, something strange happened to Julia Grant. She was in the dining room of the Willard Hotel, where they were staying. She suddenly realized that she was being rudely watched by a thin man with a moustache. Later, when she and her husband were ready to leave Washington, they got into their carriage. As they headed toward the railroad station, Julia looked out the window of the carriage. There, riding on horseback behind them, was the same man. He was staring at her.

That evening, while the Grants were headed for New Jersey, President and Mrs. Lincoln went to Ford's Theatre to see the play *Our American Cousin.* In the middle of the performance, a man named John Wilkes Booth stole into the presidential box and shot the president in the head.

Grant received a telegram with the awful news after he had arrived in Philadelphia. The Grants immediately returned to Washington, but they were not in time to see the president before he died.

General Grant and his wife were among the many mourners for the president. On the day of the funeral, Julia suddenly recalled the events of the day they had left Washington. She especially remembered the man who had followed her. Her description of him matched the description of John Wilkes Booth.

Years later, Grant and his wife admitted that they had received an anonymous letter. The writer said that he had tried and failed to shoot Grant on the train from Washington to Philadelphia. The train's porter had locked the door to Grant's car, and because of that, Grant missed being assassinated.

Grant was personally upset by the death of the president. Lincoln had been a good friend to him. He had supported him when others had complained about his drinking and his style of waging war. Lincoln had once remarked, "I think Grant has hardly a friend left, except myself."

Grant also knew of the president's goodness of heart. Lincoln had wanted to end the war and heal the nation. Grant felt that Lincoln was the best friend the South could have hoped for, because the president had not wanted to punish but rather to forgive the South.

After Lincoln's death, Vice President Andrew Johnson was sworn in as the 17th president. Unlike Lincoln, Johnson did not include in the plan of Reconstruction those Southerners who had been active in the Confederate government. "Treason is a crime and must be made odious," said Johnson. Johnson agreed with Lincoln that the best way to heal the nation was to help the South rebuild. But he still believed that Southerners of the Confederacy who had fought against their own United States government had hoped to destroy it. All those who had sided with the Confederacy during the war had to be punished, in the opinion of President Johnson.

Reconstruction—or the rebuilding of the South—had, in fact, started before the end of the war. On December 8, 1863, President Lincoln had signed the Proclamation of Amnesty and Reconstruction. This law gave a "full pardon" to Confederates who swore that they would be faithful to the United States and obey its laws. It also returned to the Confederates all their property except slaves.

Also, if in any state 10 percent of the adult white males who had voted in 1860 took the oath, they could set up a new state government. This "10 percent plan" formed the basis of Lincoln's reconstruction plan. It also caused a political fight within the Republican party.

Uniting the North and South would be a monumental task. There were some politicians in Congress, such as the Radical Republicans, who wanted to forget about the horrors of the war. To them, the war was a thing of the past. The two parts of the country should begin to live together as one. Time, they believed, would heal the wounds.

But there were many other politicians who could not forget the pain and destruction that the war had caused. They felt the South had to pay a price, that it had to prove its loyalty before being trusted as a part of the Union.

Besides Reconstruction, the other major issue after the war was freedom for African Americans. With the end of the Civil War, all the slaves in the South were freed. The 13th Amendment was added to the United States Constitution to guarantee that freedom.

There was much support in Congress for the passing of this amendment. The problem was getting the support needed to give blacks the same rights that whites had. A debate arose in Congress over this issue. For this reason, the amendment did not pass for two years. Although the 13th Amendment was introduced in Congress in December 1863, it was not officially ratified until December 1865.

Many Northerners, and Congress, did in fact support the freeing of slaves. But most of the Congress, and most of white America, had a hard time dealing with the idea that blacks would become the political equal of whites. They were not willing to treat African Americans as equal citizens, with the right to vote, own property, and so on. President Andrew Johnson held these beliefs.

The Radical Republicans, on the other hand, believed that the Civil War would have been meaningless if African Americans did not gain civil rights. This group was led by Thaddeus Stevens and Charles Sumner. The two congressmen hoped to get laws passed in Congress that would benefit African Americans. They especially hoped to get African Americans the right to vote.

President Johnson would have none of this. He vetoed laws passed by Congress concerning African-American civil rights. Johnson and the Radical Republicans became enemies.

In the early days of the Reconstruction era, Grant was not involved in this matter. Under President Johnson he had been appointed commander of the peacetime army. He was happy dealing with military matters. He did not care to get involved in politics. Johnson changed all that.

Johnson and the Radical Republicans were in constant disagreement. Some members of Johnson's own cabinet, especially Secretary of War Edwin Stanton, began siding with the Radical Republicans. The disagreement was becoming ugly.

Congress decided that President Johnson's anger was getting out of control. Many congressmen feared that the president would put an end to their work on Reconstruction and African-American rights. Congress, led by the Radical Republicans, passed several laws limiting the president's power.

The first law took away Johnson's power over the military. From the time of its passage, all military orders had to be made through the General of the Army, Ulysses Grant. A second law, the Tenure of Office Act, stated that the president could not fire anyone in his cabinet without Senate approval. It was made to protect Secretary Stanton, who had become an enemy of Johnson.

Johnson refused to follow the new laws. Johnson then acted as if Stanton had been fired. He gave the job of secretary of war to Ulysses Grant.

Grant did not care to get involved in the dispute between Congress and the president. However, he agreed to act as secretary of war until Congress could make a decision on the matter. Johnson was pleased. He took this to mean that Grant agreed with his views. He was wrong.

Grant acted as secretary of war until Congress decided that the job rightfully belonged to Stanton. Grant then resigned. Johnson became furious with Grant, and accused him of lying to him. Grant then became angry with Johnson because the president had accused him of lying.

Johnson fired Stanton a second time and named General Lorenzo Thomas as the secretary of war. Now President Johnson's troubles began to mount. In firing Stanton, he had violated the Tenure of Office Act. He had now done it a second time, and Congress felt it had no choice but to accuse him of commiting a crime. On February 24, 1868, the House of Representatives voted to impeach the president, or bring him to trial. The trial would be held by the

Senate. If the president were found guilty by two-thirds of the senators, he could be removed from office.

Andrew Johnson was the only president of the United States who had ever been impeached. Although the Senate found him not guilty, his political career was over. For the next election, the Republicans needed a new candidate for president. They looked to Ulysses Grant.

Grant was the country's greatest military hero since George Washington. He was the man who had brought victory to the North and peace to the entire country. The public saw him as honest and hard-working. He was also viewed as a man of the people, like Lincoln. He was no high-born gentleman, but a good, common man who had risen to greatness. People thought that Grant's brilliant leadership in the army would surely have prepared him to lead the country.

Grant did not seek the presidency, and he did not take steps to win it. But others were taking steps on his behalf. Grant was the most popular man in the United States. He had decided that if the people wanted him for president, he could not refuse the honor.

The Republican party nominated Grant unanimously as their candidate, and they adopted a platform that called for radical reconstruction of the South.

The Democratic nominee, Horatio Seymour, did not stand a chance. Grant won 26 out of the 34 states. He won in six Southern states, thanks largely to the enormous turnout among African Americans, who had just been given the right to vote. About 700,000 African Americans voted in the election of 1868, and almost all of them voted for Grant.

Grant had two campaign slogans during his campaign for the presidency. The most famous was "Let us have peace." A second catch phrase that he often used was "I shall have no policy of my own to interfere against the will of the people."

In November 1868, Ulysses Grant may have looked back on the recent past with amazement. Just eight years before, he had been a clerk in his father's leather goods shop. Then came the call to war, and the quick, brilliant rise through the ranks to take command of the Union armies. Now, at age 46, he was elected president of the United States. He would be one of the youngest men ever to hold that office.

14

A Troubled Presidency

"Let us have peace."

ULYSSES S. GRANT
NOMINATION SPEECH, 1868

lysses Grant believed that his election to the presidency was a "reward from the country" for his Civil War victories. It was also a great responsibility, and he took that responsibility seriously. His goal as president was to do his best to support the will of the people. His inauguration address was short and direct. He said he would support Reconstruction and pay all the government's war debts.

The country had high hopes for the new president. Some of his fellow officers, however, worried. Before Grant was even nominated for president, his close friend and associate John Rawlins hoped that he would not win the office. Rawlins said that his old friend "is not a politician or statesman—he knows how to do nothing but fight...."

However, for a time Grant's presidency went well. He signed a law insuring that the U.S. money printed during the Civil War would retain its value. He negotiated a treaty with Great Britain. The British government agreed to repay the United States for damage done the U.S. fleet by the Confederate ship *Alabama*,

The inauguration of President Grant took place at the U.S. Capitol before thousands of spectators.

which the British had built. He appointed Ely Parker, a Seneca Indian, as head of Indian affairs.

Grant thought that his biggest task as president was to put an end to the treatment of the South as an enemy. The most important chance he saw for the South was freedom for blacks. Few southern whites were happy with the fact that they had to give freedom to their slaves. Almost none of them wanted African Americans to have the right to vote. Grant felt differently. The freedom blacks had gained after the war was a great accomplishment for the entire country. But it was only the first step in a long, slow process of making African Americans equal citizens. The next step was to ensure that all African Americans had the right to vote.

That right was guaranteed by the 15th Amendment to the Constitution, which President Grant supported and which Congress passed in 1870. It stated that the right of citizens of the United States to vote could not be denied because of their race or color, or because they had once been slaves. (This amendment did not, however, give women—black or white—the right to vote. That would not come until the 19th Amendment, in 1920.)

The intentions of the 15th Amendment were good. However, they were not enough to guarantee African Americans the right to vote. Several southern states, such as Georgia and Tennessee, passed special laws, called Black Codes, to prevent African Americans from voting. One law stated that all persons had to pass a reading test in order to vote. Since most slaves had been prevented from learning to read, when they were free they could not pass the test. Another law was the "grandfather clause." According to this law, a man could vote only if his grandfather had been allowed to vote. This prevented African Americans from voting if their grandfathers had been slaves.

Laws were not the only means used in southern states to stop African Americans from voting. By 1869, a secret group called the Ku Klux Klan had come into being. The Klan used fear and violence to get their way. Klan members physically beat any African American who tried to vote. If the beatings did not work, they would burn down the house of an African American who voted, or even the church he attended. If the same person still tried to vote, the Klan used murder, usually hanging. A reign of terror had begun.

In 1870, the U.S. Department of Justice was created, and it immediately began an investigation of the Klan. In 1870 and 1871, Congress passed three bills called "force bills" to protect the rights of African Americans. Two of them said that the government could use the army to protect voting rights. In 1871, a congressional committee was formed to look into the Klan, and the Ku Klux Klan Act was passed with Grant's support. This was the third force bill. It said that troops could be used to protect civil rights.

The government sent secret agents throughout the South to find out who the members of the Klan were. These agents also kept track of Klan activities. Thousands of Klan members were found out and arrested. Many went to jail. Klan activities stopped for a time. But they eventually continued, reaching their peak in the 1920s.

Riots took place across the South, especially in Louisiana. Whites attacked blacks in hopes of putting blacks "in their place." Union troops, sent as peacekeepers, were attacked. At first President Grant did not want the army to fight back. He did not want to use more violence to stop the riots. But Grant was a military man, and he saw no other way out. He sent armed troops into the South.

This action proved to be a mistake. Southerners, as well as some Northerners, criticized Grant. He was called a tyrant who wanted complete control over the people of his country. Southerners believed he was using violence to get that control.

This was just the beginning of Grant's troubles in office. He was always more of a military man than a politician. He never felt comfortable with the presidency. His only experience was with commanding armies. He was now finding that leading a vast nation in a difficult time required very different skills.

Despite growing troubles, Grant easily won re-election in 1872. Within a short time, however, he found himself surrounded by scandal.

For Grant, the presidency was like a continuation of his military career. He gave his old army friends important government jobs, even if they did not have the needed skills or experience. He then gave directions to these men and assumed that they would follow them. But rather than pay attention to the president, many did as they pleased. Their actions finally hurt Grant.

There was much corruption in Grant's presidency. The most famous case centered around Grant's personal secretary, Orville Babcock. Babcock was one of Grant's old army friends. He was involved in a dishonest scheme known as the Whiskey Ring scandal.

The scandal was over the taxes that alcohol manufacturers were supposed to pay the government. Each year after 1870, less and less money was paid to the government in whiskey tax. This was strange, because the amount of whiskey bottled was increasing. In truth, the manufacturers paid bribes to certain people in the government. In exchange, the officials arranged for the companies to pay less tax. The government man receiving most of the bribe money was Orville Babcock.

In July 1874, a man named Benjamin Helm Bristow came to President Grant with facts that proved Babcock's guilt. Grant refused to believe them. Bristow talked to the president's staff, and they agreed that there was no doubt about Babcock's guilt. Everyone but the president thought he was guilty.

Grant went before the public and defended his secretary. More and more evidence of Babcock's guilt came to light, but still Grant would not change his mind. Eventually, the president looked like a fool. The American people wondered how a president could not be aware of such corruption on his staff. They began to doubt Grant's ability to run the country.

Grant was not used to such situations. As commander of the Union army, he had received only loyalty from his staff members. It seemed that men like Babcock changed once they were out of the army. They switched from loyalty to a leader to loyalty to money.

Grant's administration suffered from several other scandals. They were a jolt to the president. The public came to feel that Grant was someone who could be taken advantage of.

The years of his second term in office were some of the most difficult Grant had ever had to endure. One bright spot amid all the gloom was his wife, Julia. She and Grant had always remained deeply in love. In the White House, she was his comfort. Julia would sometimes interrupt his business with private notes marked "The President, Immediate." One of these notes ran:

May 22, 1875
Dear Ulysses:
    How many years ago today is it that we were engaged: Just such a
    day as this too, was it not?
                                  Julia

The President of the United States put down what he was doing and replied:

Thirty-one years ago. I was so frightened, however, that I do not remember whether it was warm or snowing.

Ulysses

The political storms that swirled around President Grant were growing more and more intense. But from time to time, inside the White House with his beloved Julia, he was able to forget about the harshness of the world outside.

Epilogue

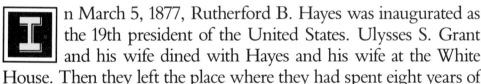n March 5, 1877, Rutherford B. Hayes was inaugurated as the 19th president of the United States. Ulysses S. Grant and his wife dined with Hayes and his wife at the White House. Then they left the place where they had spent eight years of their lives. They were now private citizens.

The end of his presidency was a great relief to Grant. Overall, the experience had not been a good one. Grant did not enjoy politics. He had started out his presidency with hope and eagerness, but, like all of his other nonmilitary experiences, it had turned into disaster.

Because Grant was a war hero, the American people overlooked a good deal of the corruption and scandals of Grant's administration. What's more, they knew that Grant himself had not been involved. As he himself said, "Failures have been errors of judgment, not of intent."

Grant had saved a few thousand dollars from his presidential salary. After leaving Washington, he and his family set out for a trip around the world. They left the United States in May 1877. For the next two and a half years they visited many countries.

MRS. U. S.   MRS. NELLIE   GENERAL   COLONEL FREDERICK D. GRANT,   JESSE R. GRANT,
  GRANT   GRANT SARTORIS   U. S. GRANT   ELDEST SON   YOUNGEST SON

COPYRIGHT, 1911, REVIEW OF REVIEWS CO.

U. S. GRANT, JR.,   JULIA GRANT,   ULYSSES   IDA HONORÉ   NELLIE   MRS. ELIZABETH
    THE   DAUGHTER   S. GRANT,   GRANT,   GRANT,   C. GRANT,
   SECOND   OF   THIRD SON OF   WIFE OF   DAUGHTER OF   WIFE OF
    SON   F. D. GRANT   F. D. GRANT   F. D. GRANT   JESSE R. GRANT   JESSE R. GRANT

After his retirement, General Grant was often joined by a host of family members.

England, Germany, China, Russia, Japan, and Egypt were a few of the stops on Grant's world tour. Everywhere he went, crowds gathered to show him their respect and to get a glimpse of the hero of the American Civil War. The people thought of him as the great American general, not as the president who had failed.

The tour ended in 1879. Grant and his wife returned to the United States and moved to New York City. Grant had very little money, but at this time some wealthy admirers gave him a donation of $250,000. He decided to invest the money. Grant's son, Buck, along with a man named Ferdinand Ward, had opened the brokerage firm of Grant & Ward. The firm traded in elevated railroad stock. Buck talked his father into investing $100,000 in the company.

Once again, Grant was destined for failure. Ferdinand Ward had gone into business with Buck in order to make money using the famous Grant name. He did not care how he went about doing so. He took money from the firm and used it for himself. Eventually, the firm collapsed, and Grant lost his entire investment.

The loss put Grant on the verge of bankruptcy. He was not able to pay his bills. Once again, he had trouble surviving. History was repeating itself. Just as it had happened long ago, Grant was on the road to poverty. It was as if he had never been a famous general or a president of the United States. The hard times were back again.

A number of publishers asked Grant if he would be interested in writing magazine articles describing his wartime experiences. Writing was a way for Grant to make ends meet. In 1884 he published an article on the Battle of Shiloh in the *Century Magazine*. He did not like the idea of selling his memories of the Civil War, but he needed the money.

That same year Grant received another offer. The novelist Mark Twain, author of *The Adventures of Tom Sawyer* and *Huckleberry Finn*, asked Grant to consider writing a book about his wartime experiences. Twain said that his publisher would pay Grant handsomely for such a book.

Grant had been depressed. His financial situation recalled the hard days in St. Louis, when he had to sell firewood on the streets. What's more, he had recently learned that he had throat cancer. He was in pain and did not know how much longer he would live.

He accepted the book offer and gradually became caught up in the task of writing his story of the Civil War.

The project was to be a two-volume history entitled *Personal Memoirs*. Grant looked upon it as a way to present his view of the battles and decisions of the war. Grant wrote feverishly during 1884 and 1885. His condition became worse, but still he wrote. He was racing with death.

Two days after he had completed his last chapter, Grant died. The book was a great success in two ways: It told Grant's story of the Civil War, and it provided for his family. Julia received $400,000 in royalty income from sales of the book.

This photo of Grant writing his memoirs was taken four weeks before he died.

Grant died on July 23, 1885. Around the country people mourned the passing of the great war hero. His life had been a very full one. He had seen very good times, and he had experienced bad ones as well. He had known what it was like to be penniless and desperate. He had also known enormous popularity and great power. Failure and success were equally familiar to him.

It is true Grant had difficult times in civilian life. Trouble always seemed to come to him when he was outside the military. From an early age, he had shown a capacity for strategy and the tactics of warfare. His great work in life was leading men into battle. Anything he did outside of the military seemed to end in disaster, but whatever he did in the military ended in glorious success. In a way, that was to be expected. Ulysses S. Grant was a soldier, first and last.

TIMETABLE OF EVENTS IN THE LIFE OF
ULYSSES S. GRANT

April 27, 1822	Born in Point Pleasant, Ohio
1839–43	Attends West Point
1844	Begins duty as a second lieutenant in the US Army
1846–48	Leads his first troops in the Mexican War
1848	Marries Julia Dent
1852	Transferred to Fort Vancouver in the Oregon Territory
1854	Resigns from the US Army
1861	The Civil War breaks out; Grant joins the army
1862	Promoted to major general Captures Ft. Henry and Ft. Donelson
1863	Wins Battle of Chattanooga, Tennessee Captures Vicksburg, Tennessee
1864	Appointed general-in-chief of all Union forces
1864–65	Harasses Robert E. Lee's army in the Wilderness Campaign
1865	Accepts Lee's surrender at Appomattox Court House, Virginia
1868	Elected president of the United States
1877	After leaving office, goes on a world tour
July 23, 1885	Dies on July 23

SELECTED SOURCES

ULYSSES S. GRANT

Carpenter, John A. *Ulysses S. Grant*. New York: Twayne Publishers, 1970.

Catton, Bruce. *Grant and the Military Tradition*. Boston: Little, Brown and Co., 1954.

Catton, Bruce. *Grant Moves South*. Boston: Little, Brown and Co., 1960.

Catton, Bruce. *Grant Takes Command*. Boston: Little, Brown and Co., 1968.

Grant, Ulysses S. *Personal Memoirs*. New York: Da Capo Press, 1983.

Johnson, Allen, and Dumas Malone. *Dictionary of American Biography*. New York: Charles Scribner's Sons, 1931–32.

McFeely, William S. *Grant: A Biography*. New York: W.W. Norton & Co., 1981.

Wilson, David L., and John Y. Simon. *Ulysses S. Grant: Essays and Documents*. Carbondale: Southern Illinois University Press, 1981.

THE CIVIL WAR

Baker, Alan. *The Civil War in America*. New York: Anchor Books, 1961.

Beringer, Richard E., Herman Hattaway, Archer Jones, and William N. Still, Jr. *Why the South Lost the Civil War*. Athens: University of Georgia Press, 1986.

Bowman, John S. *The Civil War Almanac*. New York: Bison Books, 1982.

Hattaway, Herman, and Archer Jones. *How the North Won: A Military History of the Civil War*. Chicago: University of Illinois Press, 1983.

McPherson, James M. *Ordeal By Fire: The Civil War and Reconstruction*. New York: Alfred A. Knopf, 1982.

SUGGESTED READING

Falkof, Lucille. *Ulysses S. Grant: 18th President of the United States*. Ada, Okla.: Garret Education Corp., 1988.

Kent, Zachary. *Ulysses S. Grant*. Chicago: Childrens Press, 1989.

Meyer, Howard N. *Let Us Have Peace*. New York: Crowell–Collier, 1966.

Nolan, Jeanette. *The Story of Ulysses S. Grant*. New York: Grosset and Dunlap, 1952.

*Pitkin, Thomas M., ed. *Grant, the Soldier*. Washington: Acropolis Books, 1965.

Smith, Gene. *Lee and Grant: A Dual Biography*. New York: New American Library, 1984.

Viola, Herman J. *Ulysses S. Grant*. New York: Chelsea House, 1990.

Williams, T. Harry. *Lincoln and His Generals*. New York: Grosset & Dunlap, 1952.

*Young, Bob. *Reluctant Warrior: Ulysses S. Grant*. New York: Julian Messner, 1971.

Zadra, Dan. *Statesmen in America: Ulysses S. Grant*. Mankato, Minn.: Creative Education, 1988.

*Readers of *Ulysses S. Grant and the Strategy of Victory* will find these books particularly readable.

INDEX

Laura Ann Rickarby is an instructor at the University of Maryland in Baltimore, Maryland. She has also taught American history at Hunter College and Baruch College in New York City. Ms. Rickarby is currently completing her doctoral work in American history at Columbia University.